Ironic Witness

Ironic Witness

Diane Glancy

WIPF & STOCK · Eugene, Oregon

IRONIC WITNESS

Copyright © 2015 Diane Glancy. All rights reserved. Except for brief quotations in critical publications or reviews, no part of this book may be reproduced in any manner without prior written permission from the publisher. Write: Permissions. Wipf and Stock Publishers, 199 W. 8th Ave., Suite 3, Eugene, OR 97401.

Wipf & Stock
An Imprint of Wipf and Stock Publishers
199 W. 8th Ave., Suite 3
Eugene, OR 97401

www.wipfandstock.com

ISBN 13: 978-1-62564-744-3

Manufactured in the U.S.A.   04/14/2015

I would like to thank my writers' group at Azusa Pacific University: Christine Kern, Thomas Albaugh, Katie Manning, Luba Zakharov

Contents

The Visit | 1
My Work | 12
Soundings | 15
At Its Deadliest | 19
Sparses | 22
Several Nights after Daniel Died | 28
What Is There in Ziggurats That Words Cannot Say? | 30
A Ziggurat Is a Funeral Umbrella | 33
Ziggurats Are a Figmentor of Imagination | 35
If I Start to Nap, I Growl | 38
Casting Doubt | 41
What Had I Understood? | 42
The Spiral of the Galaxy—the Spiral of My Ziggurats | 44
A Freak Snow | 49
Grounding | 53
The Prophecies of Ziggurats | 55

Daniel's Visions | 62
A Collapse | 64
Lot's Wife | 67
Rock City | 70
Flaw | 71
Daniel's Funeral | 73
Back Flash | 75
A Brief Confrontation | 82
Ironic Witness | 84
The Blue Scarf | 87
Off the Road | 90
Uncle John Winscott's Funeral | 93
Frank's Years in the Ministry | 97
Frank's Death | 99
Another Visit to the Cemetery | 102
Wired | 104
A Sign on the Road | 105
In Hell There Is No Night | 118

Contents

Fragments Came to Me and Patterned Themselves as Ziggurats | 121

How Could A Minister's Wife Be Found in Hell? | 129

Far | 131

Daniel in Hell | 133

Ziggurats for Sale | 135

Frank in Heaven | 148

What I was living, that I am dead.
—Dante Alighieri, *Inferno*, canto 14

I don't want to be a tree, I want to be its meaning.
—Orhan Pamuk, *My Name Is Red*

And the whole earth was of one language and one speech.

And it came to pass, as they journeyed from the east, that they found a plain in the land of Shinar; and they dwelt there.

And they said one to another, "Come, let us make brick, and burn them thoroughly." And they had brick for stone, and slime for mortar.

And they said, "Come, let us build a city and a tower, whose top may reach heaven."

And the Lord came down to see the city and the tower, which they had built.

And the Lord said, "Behold, the people are one, and they have one language. Nothing will be withheld from them that they imagined to do. Come, let us go down, and confound their language."

So the Lord went down and scattered them upon the face of the earth and they stopped building.

—Gen 11:1–9, KJV

The Visit

ANOTHER LETTER FROM THE afterlife, you might say. But this one starts before the afterlife and continues into it. I would implore you to make the effort. It's for you, as much as for me—maybe more, for eventually, I am no longer in the place you call *here*.

At first, there was distancing of what I knew. There was Frank's death. Daniel's before that. The sound of the mower in our yard. The buzzing, always buzzing, at the window of my work shed. I think Daniel mowed because he needed the repetition—going back and forth over the same ground. Other times, a friend of Daniel's mowed while Daniel stood in the drive and watched him as if part of his mind were caught there in the mowing.

Daniel was not our only child. We have two other children, Winifred and Warren. But Daniel was the focus, and all that followed him. I leaned on Frank, my husband, a retired minister and professor of biblical studies, as we traveled through the turmoil of the Daniel years.

Christianity. The sweet tangle of my life. I could shred it with my teeth. It was ever before me. As a young woman, I married a minister. Forty-two years later, what did I expect? Certainly not a son staked on drugs. Dead on arrival with an ear chewed by broken glass or an animal in the night, and an assurance from Frank, my husband, that Daniel was in heaven because he'd accepted Christ as a boy, though Christ was never a consideration to Daniel as far as I knew. Daniel seemed never to stop running from him. Or he acted like he wasn't there at all. I expected Frank to say, "like his mother" in his despair, though he never did. Did Frank blame me and my indifference to what he preached? He never said so to my face, even when he went in by himself to identify Daniel's gobbled body. It was a holy calling—a calling of the holy Christ to bear up as Frank did. It was as if Daniel, our son, had had enough and would spare himself and us further exasperation, and begging, and warning, and failure after failure, and use and reuse and reuse until we knew it would not change, not even by a blazing miracle of a high God, though I'm sure Frank held out hope to the end. Daniel wouldn't have been in my heaven for all the grief he caused.

This is about the terror I faced. Evident in the weather—in attacks of other sorts, both from inside and out—in attacks of despair—in attacks of terrorists—in attacks of aging, which are terrorists in themselves.

I can look back at myself and say, "a gulf separates us." Often I retreated into my work as if the upheaval could be terminated in the kiln, where I fired the clay as if it was the circumstances Daniel handed to us.

I was a maker of ziggurats. I shaped clay into the likenesses of ziggurats. I was a maker of their clay forms. The various gradations that climbed from them. I worked mainly with shape. There's an edginess that comes when I'm working—a vision of sorts—a zigzag line or the jump of a lightning bolt, jagged as the jaws of life and as disconcerting as tearing a car open to extricate what is caught there.

I kept journals of my work on ziggurats in my work shed, which I titled, *The Ziggurat Journals*, or *Ziggurats and Me*, volumes 1 through 7. I was now in my eighth journal. All of them massive, sagging the shelves in my work shed where they sat. Sometimes I spent more time writing notes on the making of ziggurats than I did on the actual making of the ziggurats. The journals were about how I stepped into what I think now was hell—or the beginning of it.

From the start, Daniel showed up in my journals.

Journal entry, May 2: *I hear Daniel on the stairs at night. I hear him in the yard. I think he's talking to someone I can't see.*

"If you hadn't named him Daniel—a man crazy with visions," I said to Frank when we visited the cemetery with a bundle of wildflowers. Daniel, who died in a car accident at thirty-eight, zagged on drugs, as he had been for years.

"I saw a vision that made me afraid, and the thoughts on my bed and visions in my head troubled me," Frank said. "From Dan 4:5, the twenty-seventh chapter of the Old Testament."

I took Frank's arm as we walked back to the car. My accusation wasn't a reproach as much as a manner of conversation between us.

"Daniel in the Bible survived his visions, unlike our Daniel," Frank said as we drove back to our place, and I returned to my work shed.

Journal entry, May 23: *I write to you foreclawed in Christ our Lord.*

Sometimes, I read to Frank at the breakfast table before I went to my work shed. His eyes were not what they had been, and he read most of the day on his own, often with a magnifying glass. I started with the Bible that was not his favorite translation.

"'You keep my eyelids from closing' (Ps 77:4)," I read from the New Revised Standard Version.

Frank looked at his Bible. "'You hold my eyes waking,'" Frank said. "That's the King James Version, the one I prefer."

"It means I can't sleep because of your snoring, your voyages at night. The troubled waters of your sleep. You call out from your rowing. I can't sleep, Frank. I think I'm moving to the other room."

"Hopefully, Winnie or Warren won't return."

"It happens."

"Yes, more all the time. But it doesn't look like ours will be back soon," Frank said. "They'd give us warning if they were coming."

"They just have."

"When?"

"I opened the e-mail before I fixed breakfast," I said.

"For a visit or permanent?" he asked.

"A visit."

"Short or long?"

"Winnie didn't say," I said.

"You didn't ask?" he questioned.

"I haven't answered her," I said.

"Don't make it seem like they aren't welcome, or that we're wondering how soon after their arrival they'll leave," he said. "What's the purpose of their visit?"

"To see us. To make sure we're all right. To see if we need to be put away. I'll get Mrs. Woodruff to clean before they come."

"You're the only woman I know who calls her help by her formal name," Frank said.

"I'll have Edna Woodruff clean the house, so they know we're still with it."

"Don't make them too comfortable."

"Don't drive them away too soon with your ranting," I told him. "If they think you're off, they might stay to corral you into some sort of reasonable presentation of yourself."

"I won't scare them."

"I don't know why it's so hard for you to make yourself presentable," I said.

"Because I'm looking at the lightings," Frank continued, with his nose glued to his Bible. "'His lightings lightened the world; the earth saw it and trembled' (Ps 97:4, KJV)."

I looked at the Bible. "His lightnings, Frank. Not lightings."

"I misread that for a purpose," he said. "I wasn't thinking of lights in the heavens. I was thinking of the lightings of the Word. I think God speaks with fire. There's a physical light of sorts in the biblical language. I think I see it at night. I dream sometimes there's a bright light blinding me. Each reading is a visit from God. In Scripture, there was light before there was the sun. There's a mystery there."

"Your children don't like to hear your emanations," I said. "I wouldn't have them while they're here. Our independence depends on their assurance that we're still functioning. You can't go on about his lightings lighting the world. You sound like you've not quite landed this morning."

"No, I haven't," he agreed. "But it's not from a voyage. It's from somewhere in flight."

"Don't I know it."

"You won't be moving from the room until after the children leave?" he asked.

"No, maybe not then—if you'd stop your snoring."

Once, I had asked Winnie and Warren how they had been affected by Daniel's death. They were sorry, they said. They still grieved for him. As the oldest, Daniel had been the front-runner. They were closer in age, more friends with one another than Daniel. He had been absent for years. If he

THE VISIT

came to the house, he was distant, already disengaged from the family. Finally, his visits were dreaded. Winnie and Warren remembered him in his own world, even as a child.

"What does a passage mean in relationship to what came before and after it? What is riding on it?" Frank asked that evening. I wasn't sure if he was talking to himself or me. Maybe Frank was addressing us both. "We're not dealing with an ordinary house made of beams and timbers and walls and windows. What roof does righteousness have? What shingles cover justice?" He sat at the table, hardly tasting the dinner I had made—roast lamb with gravy he always liked. It had been work. Could there be a conversation? No, it was a one-way street, if there was a street there at all. Had he been working on the same passage all day? But hadn't I been with the same ziggurat all day in my shed?

"What does that mean, 'His lightings lighted the world'?" Frank continued. "The stars. The suns. The moons. The comets and meteors. The fire-tails of their frictions. How is it applicable to us here in our little lives? In our studies? At our tables and desks? In our work sheds? At our books? What hope is there that we could understand?"

I called him back from despair with news. "You misread the words, Frank. It's hard enough when you read biblical language correctly. How much harder when you don't?"

But he considered it a divinely inspired mistake. A misreading of the highest order. He would spend the evening and the next several days seeking the meaning of that mistake. Where was it guiding him?

I looked at the photographs of our three children, Daniel, Winnie, and Warren, as I listened to Frank. They were on the wall behind him, with their wild Winscott hair and freckled noses.

"When you say 'lightings,' you make it sound like the heavens are wired with electricity and God just throws a switch and there is light."

"I don't want the children hearing our arguments over semantics," Frank said.

"I don't want them hearing us argue at all," I insisted.

"If you want to argue, let's make it something that counts."

"Let's argue over the pile of leaves you leave in the yard," I told him. "Maybe Mrs. Woodruff's husband or son would rake for us. Maybe I'll get out there while she cleans the house. Maybe I'll do your work for you. Let the children see that."

"Eugena—" He used my full name. Not Gena or Jean. Not Euge, which reminds me of "huge," which I am not. Or any of his other words for me. Leaving me to figure out exactly what he meant—leaving my name hanging in the air.

———

I was a maker of clay figures. I was caught up in the ziggurat—making likenesses of Dante's nine rings of the *Inferno*. The tower of Babel also was a ziggurat, upright as the Guggenheim Museum in New York City, though the Guggenheim is inverted, its smaller rings growing larger as it climbs. Other ziggurats started larger and became smaller as they ascended. Dante's *Inferno* began with the larger rings and became smaller as they descended. The tower of Babel and the *Inferno* would make a palindrome, if the ziggurats were language.

Most of my ziggurats did not even look like ziggurats. They were my interpretation. My indirect approach. What a ziggurat was at its essence. Its abstraction. Its meaning. There was something about the word I loved.

The brain is amazing. It is a ziggurat that cannot be penetrated. It can hide a city inside it. The coils of the brain are gray ropes of clay worked together, inextricable as a body wrapped around the broken pieces of a car. I was the shaper of those clay forms. The maker of larger rings growing smaller as they ascended—or descended to the pit of Dante's *Inferno*, as if ropes let down to retrieve Daniel, a son who took our love for him and turned it into fury so malformed that no one guessed it could be love.

———

I was in my work shed behind the house working with another form when I heard the car.

It couldn't be the children. They weren't scheduled to arrive for several hours.

I returned to my clay, knowing Frank could answer the door. It was probably someone for him anyway.

At dawn, the side of a shed in the distance reflected the morning sun. Otherwise, during the day, I didn't know the shed was there. It disappeared among the trees in the woods. By afternoon, in the other direction, the sun moved toward the west, shooting its light backwards across a field. It was then that I watched the rows of crops and pasturelands. Sometimes I marked my ziggurats with their rows. Usually, I worked until I could look at the trees in the yard and know they were tired after holding up their arms all day. Sometimes the different rungs of the circles of my ziggurats caught my attention as I passed there, maybe the way Dante stopped to take note of who was in the rings of his inferno and why.

I heard Frank call my name, irritated enough that I knew it had not been his first call. Our visitor was Edwin Harsler, an old friend of ours who had been recently widowed. He made a habit of driving around the country, stopping at houses where he knew people. Ours must have been the house of the day, but I was at work with my clay and didn't want to leave. Frank called again.

I didn't want to stop work. I felt inhospitable. When I passed through those moods, I felt a sourness I didn't feel otherwise. Spaces appeared in the ziggurats I didn't know were there.

I went to the house and found Edwin at the table with Frank. The coffee pot was empty. Frank could have made more coffee, but he used it as an excuse to call me.

"How are you, Edwin?"

"Fine," he answered. "I was on my way to town when I passed."

"I'm glad you stopped." What was I saying? Was that me or Frank who spoke? It was me, I saw by Frank's eyes. He was enjoying seeing me uncomfortable at the interruption. He liked the way I covered my feelings.

"My daughter's coming for a visit. I wonder if you'd drop by."

"Our children are coming also," I said. "Why don't you and Helen come by here and we'll all have dinner and catch up?"

That must have been what he was looking for, because he seemed pleased.

"She's bringing someone with her. A young man she's been dating."

"Is it serious?"

"I don't know, but I suspect it is. She doesn't usually bring anyone with her. Or if she does, it's been girlfriends."

"Winnie used to bring boys, but none of them ever seem to come back," I said.

"You think it's us?" Frank asked. "After they see the mess in my study and your clay infernos covering every open space in our house, they must find excuses to make an exit."

"Yes, it's harder to get married these days," Edwin said. "The young are not so anxious. Or they take longer. To make sure, I suppose."

"How are you doing, Edwin?" Frank asked. "There're widows at every turn."

I looked at Frank. When had he begun noticing widows? And what widows was he noticing?

He looked away.

"Yes, I've been invited to dinner several times. I've found a basket of biscuits on my doorstep. Saide doesn't bark any more when the women leave a casserole on my porch or stop to slip an invitation in the mailbox."

Was Frank wishing he could ride with Edwin past all the mailboxes, reviewing the names of widows of men who had passed on?

I returned to my work shed when Edwin left.

Our children: Winifred and Warren—the two who were left from the three.

Winnie came to me once saying she hated her name. Winnie Winscott. Why not Minnie Mascot?

I apologized for the cuteness. It seemed all right when she was small. But now?

"Well, call yourself by your full name—Winifred Winscott."

"No."

"Is it the alliteration?"

"Of course it is. Didn't you know I would grow up to be an adult?"

"Yes, Winifred, I did. But when you were born, I had Frank's parents standing over me and Grandma Winifred, of course, who wanted you named after her, just as she had been named after her grandmother."

"But Winscott wasn't her last name until she married. You should have refused."

"Change your name," I said.

"You should have insisted."

"They were a formidable group," I told her. "Blame your father. They were his relatives."

"I didn't know you were so spineless."

"I have a spine. I didn't mind the name. Winifred Eugena Winscott. Is it my name also to which you object?"

"No, it's hidden between the two Ws," she said. "I hardly know it's there. You could have been more original."

"Warren doesn't complain about his name," I reminded her.

"Because Warren Winscott isn't as ruffled as Winnie Winscott."

"I get your point. When you have a daughter, you can name her something removed from family ties. When you marry, you can take your husband's name."

"It would entice me to marry," she said.

"I hope his name is Willets."

There were times after Daniel died when I went through my blue mood. When I passed that place, which was most of the time, I felt things I didn't feel otherwise. It was like that shed in the distance that only appeared when the morning sun passed over the hill.

One of the reasons I dreaded the children's return was that they would leave again, taking Daniel with them also. Now I waited for another visit, suiting up to feel the loss of Daniel again. Why couldn't I just appreciate the two children I had left?

The weather was often unpredictable, and we had waited in airports for hours for their arrival, sometimes making the long drive back home in rain or snow after canceled flights. Now Warren and Winnie rented a car. We began having our Christmas in July. The children would arrive with presents, unwrapped because of airline regulations.

I stayed in my work shed until I heard their car in the drive. I also stayed in the shed when they left.

I had been the mother of three children, still was. The death of a child didn't remove him from being a child.

One morning, I woke with a dream that a bat had flown to the side of my head. I pulled it off and put it on the ground. I saw that it was wounded. In my dream, I actually saw the open, bleeding wounds that are drug addiction. The undercurrent of whispered names that unthreaded the structure of a family.

What had I done wrong? Nothing. Nothing. It was Daniel's fault. He was responsible for his own addiction. There were days when I was tired of children. After I fed them, after we played, after they napped, what was there still to do? Prepare dinner. By then they were restless and fighting. I bathed them, read to them, got them in bed. When I heard their feet on the stairs, I yelled at them to get back in bed. Sometimes I was in tears, as they were. If Frank was at a meeting, or visiting one of the members of the church, or traveling to a conference somewhere, the weight of the whole house was on my shoulders. I sat in the large, overstuffed chair in Frank's study, too tired to do anything I wanted to do. Upstairs, Winnie and Warren eventually went to sleep, but Daniel must have sat in the darkness before an enormous emptiness that he later filled with drugs. Already, another day with the children was on its way, then another, and another. It was not my fault. I did what I could do. I did more than I could do. I was bored with the routine of housework, but I kept at it. Often, I only wanted my own work, which would have to wait for years and years, or at least until the children were in school, when I could have time in my work shed with my ziggurats, unless Frank insisted I take the women's Bible study or some other function at the church as the minister's wife.

Daniel never left, and therefore never returned for a visit as Winnie and Warren did. If Daniel returned, it was for an assault. Often, I thought I heard Daniel's car pass in the night. Often, I thought he slept in his car at the end of the drive. Often, I dreaded him entering the house.

Edwin, his daughter, Helen, and her friend, Jake, came for dinner one evening as we had planned. Helen and Winnie had been friends, though Helen was a year older and in a different class in high school. We went to the same church, and they were in the youth group together. Warren was two years younger than Winnie. The children talked of their careers, the demands of city living, of the war, politics, the economy, and other turbulent events in the world. Edwin, Frank, and I listened, amused that we had taken a backseat. They were now the parents, and we were the children. Once in a while, they stopped to ask our opinion—just to be polite, to include others, as they had been taught. Or Frank would interrupt with some information they would consider irrelevant, just to irritate them—just to see how they could recover from his statement and continue their conversation. I glared at him once. Jake had lost his job and was looking again after a short period of dejection. Winnie was worried about her job. Helen and Jake seemed comfortable with their standing at work, "though no one really knows security anymore," Winnie said. We lived in a tenuous world at best.

That was something Grandma Winifred could have said, though I didn't tell Winnie.

The men began another conversation. Edwin was listening to Frank's latest insight into translation. Jake was listening to Warren. Helen and Winnie were talking also, but listening at the same time to the boys and trying to pull them into their own conversation. I was listening to the children's conversation and noticing a cycle, a circling up or down from a previous comment. They were making ziggurats, though they wouldn't want that information either. When had I grown so limited in what I could say? But they were unaware of how often they circled up or down from the same place. Maybe they were aware of it also. Helen seemed to pull them away for a moment, but ultimately was unsuccessful. There was something in their pattern of speech that assured them of their place. Even Jake was aware that he was beginning a new beginning. Looking for another job that would take him in a new direction. He had to follow trends. He had to adjust. Be pliable. No, that wasn't the word. Able to adapt. There, that was the word. His depression was on the mend. Dejection, he corrected Helen.

Helen was in retail at Millworth's, a high-end department store. She invited Winnie to the city. She could stay in her apartment. They could see plays and visit museums. Winnie decided she would like that. Their acquaintance could be renewed. If old friendships could be revived. That would give Edwin more excuse to stop by when he was in the neighborhood, though we had no neighbors and lived on a road that only went farther into the country. He had to be on his way nowhere to drive by our house. Or taking a convoluted way to town by which he had to turn around or back up for some distance. He would bring news of the girls' adventures in the city, though Winnie had a cell phone and we often talked.

"What about Helen Harsler?" I asked Winnie when they left. "Do you think she hates her name?"

"Was it an epidemic?"

"What?"

"Naming daughters with the letters that began their last names."

My Work

MY WORK SHED WAS open to the public—my clay figures for sale. But a car rarely came. I left a billet in the bed-and-breakfast in Fenton. Sometimes several women who had come to a little inn in town for lunch would venture up the road. I think they were puzzled by my work, and they would politely found a way to leave.

I was a maker of clay, I reminded myself. No, the clay was made. I was a maker of clay figures. A maker in clay. I worked for years before I had a showing. But Daniel, in the Old Testament, in exile all his life, still made his prophecies. I felt my clay figures were prophecies. Sometimes I felt my audience was God, despite the self-imposed distance I felt from him.

Actually, I'm afraid of prophecy. It's a risk. Even more than working with clay. No one paid attention anyway, Frank said. No one understood the underworkings, or the meaning of my ziggurats. That's another reason working with clay is a kind of prophecy. I could send all kinds of indirect and hidden messages. No one would pay attention. I remembered Frank's words.

Some days, I worked on formation. Some days, I only wrote about the formation. I'm sure God likes art. He's the author of it. I recognize what he can do when I see the evening clouds he shapes into ziggurats.

I've always suspected heaven is something of an art gallery. A living gallery. A living galaxy in which everything breathes and has voice and moves at will. How would I explain hell when I found it? Little pieces of information fell now and then, even before I was there. It mainly had to do with the darkness of my own despair and the death of our son, Daniel. But I could push it away with a new ziggurat called *Lightings*.

"I guess you think they pay attention to your translations," I said.

You would think the anguish would dissipate and the sorrow lessen. But I continued to wound. I like to go back and remember the land, because it is the origin of clay. In those moments, I was not tormented. I liked the winter landscape. The earth was not as *covered* as it was in summer.

Though I was in my blue period, it was all the browns that held me. The leafless trees. The russet edges of the fields. The dried grasses. Even the sky seemed brown along the horizon with a storm that passed in the north. I think that's what I'll miss about the earth when I'm no longer here. I'll sit under the upper edge of hell, with my little blowhole that lets in cool air, and think about the loveliness I knew on earth.

Hell is the absence of God. The separation from God. I had heard that from Frank all our married life. If I stayed separate from him in this life, he would stay separate from me in the hereafter. It was my choice.

Maybe the browns were calling me out of the blue period several years after Daniel's death. Wasn't it time I moved on?

I liked abandoned farmhouses with their gray weathered clapboards open to the air, windows gone, the wide sky invading the boards of the roof. In a few years, the old roof would collapse into the house.

There also was a sign reading "Jesus is Lord" on the side of a shed. I remember thinking, What did that mean? I had come from a non-religious family. Maybe that was my rebellion. I would become a follower of this puzzling man, all wingspread and wrapped in conflict, with a crown of barbed wire like you see sometimes draped over a fencepost.

The cemetery pines were the only green leftover from summer—the only reminder the land would not always be brown.

I liked the hay rolls. The windbreaks between fields. A hawk in a bare tree. Even the vapor trails crisscrossing the sky.

In the end, I wasn't much of a rebel. I was a crone, a hawk on a leafless tree, barely holding on against the wind. The blue mood stayed with me as a bird. No—a bat. It rested in my hair. Its wings up-tipped in the wind.

The country I knew as a child visiting my grandfather's farm had diminished. It was invisible, actually. I could tell my children what it was like in my memory, as I did when the lights went out in a storm, but they could not really understand. Sometimes they seemed bored as I talked, only listening out of politeness. They could know it happened—that I was a child on a farm in a different world than the one they knew, but they could not know it. I could say it was all a matter of perception, or experience, actually—or perception that comes through experience. Otherwise, it is someone else's tale.

Do you know there were times we ran in the fields and played in the potato cellar and climbed on the tin roof of the pig shed? There was the barn. The pond in the field. Grandfather Nyland walking behind his horse in the distance. The farmhouse, with its kerosene lamp in the darkness as soon as the sun went down. No news from anywhere. Nothing from nowhere. All was isolation on a farm. The whole world. The heat. The cold. The water pump at the kitchen sink. The pantry. The black hole of the attic. All of it gone.

They did not understand the absence of electricity. It was there, they said. It had always existed. Yes, but we didn't know how to connect with it. Or my grandparents didn't. We had it at our parent's house in town, but wires had not reached the farm. How could I expect them to understand?

Soundings

A ZIGGURAT IS AN ancient tower made by Assyrians and Babylonians in the form of a terraced pyramid with each story smaller than the one under it. Also called *zikkurat, zikurat,* and *zigguratu,* meaning height or pinnacle. That is from the dictionary. But a ziggurat is an inverted jar in which insects crawl. When I look closer, the insects are human. Beyond them, but still inside the jar—a plane full of people unaware of one another, all wanting out, but there is no way. That was my *Moanings-in-Hell* piece.

I have to remember I had a chance to change. I knew there was a way I should follow, but I did not. I could babble as I wished in clay. *The Plain of Shinar* was my first piece that had a showing. Frank placed it on a table in the basement of the church before a fellowship dinner. It was met with mixed reviews. Shinar was the place where the Tower of Babel was built (Gen 11:2).

It was the death of our first son, Daniel, that led to other titles: *Let the Day Perish* (Job 3:3). *The Waters Close over Me* (Jonah 2:5). *If I Go into the Pit, Who Will Praise You?* (Ps 30:9). *Why Have You Cast Me off?* (Ps 43:2).

I had terrible dreams before Daniel died. I knew it would happen before it did, and I was helpless before it. Ziggurats were falling. Once, I heard them shriek.

Addiction is a dye that seeps everywhere.

We had a party once, and I invited a clown who bothered the guests more than he entertained. I finally asked him to leave. I forgot the neighbors had a dog they let roam at night. We heard the dog growl after the clown left. We heard a commotion. When we called the dog to the door, it had clown fabric in its teeth. In hell, it is flesh that the dogs have in their mouths.

We got together on Sunday evenings and read *The Divine Comedy*. Frank, my husband, had a circle of friends. It was Frank who called the meetings, but I gladly went along with it. John Winscott, Frank's uncle, was the other constant. Thelma, his wife, came also. She kept an eye on the children—Daniel, Winnie, Warren, and her three, John II, Lizbet, and Thomas.

"This is not a comedy. It's heaven's revenge on us for not paying attention. Ignoring it. Or mixing it with other messages," I heard them say as I listened. "God does not share his kingdom with anything that is not his."

A ziggurat has altitude. Elevation. There's a pitch to it. A style. If a ziggurat was an animal, it would be the giraffe. But that's too easy. If it had depth, it would be a copper mine in the Arizona desert.

Hypsography is the measure of altitude. Other words are altimetry. Hypsometer. Altimeter. Summit. Cloud-capped. The opposite is lowness. Depression. Pit. Shaft. Cavity. Abyss. Crevasse. Infernal pit. Subterranean. Abysmal. I still like to read the thesaurus and dictionary. I like to warp the forms of my ziggurats.

I was always making *soundings*. One reason I liked ziggurats is that they contained both. These oppositions were what I used in my art. It was Jack and the old story of the beanstalk. Ziggurats are both horizontal and vertical. You feel like you're walking on a level plane—well, maybe you feel the slight gradation, but you are rising, or descending, if you turn around—and you are at a different level before you realize it.

It is possible that the earth itself is a symbol of the shape of the afterlife. It is hot in the center, and the sky is cold above it. The earth is the settling point. The platform of decision—that's what I would call life on earth.

Does speaking on one's own always have to mean Babel? Does God knock buildings down, as we did to one another as children?

Many religions are a ziggurat—an attempt to reach God by one's own hands. I will not make many friends saying that. But I don't think they want to be friends. They are like the neighbor's dog after dark. And we are the clowns. Don't they already have some cloth from our clown suit in their teeth?

"We are broken before God, who had a Son he sent to the cross to become broken for our sins," Frank continued as he always did. "He did the work. He is the tower. The upward path to heaven. All others go downward on the inverted ziggurat of their own making."

"That's enough to start a war," I said.

"More than enough," Frank answered.

I believed my life was in my breaking before him.

"But haven't Christians been terrorists in the past?" I asked Frank. "Maybe still are."

I am not a prophet, even with my ziggurats. But sometimes I listen to Scripture when Frank and John Winscott talk, and there, in a little wormhole, I find the universe.

I believe each believer believes in their own way.

These things have I spoken unto you, that you should not be made to stumble. They will put you out of the synagogues; yes, the time is coming that when whoever kills you will think that he does God a service. And these things will they do unto you, because they have not known the Father, nor me. But these things have I told you, that when the time comes, you may remember that I told you of them.

—JOHN 16:1–4

"You've got a scary book there, Frank," I said when I heard Frank and his uncle John Winscott discussing the passage. I tried to ignore them, but it seemed to me a possibility of what could be ahead—in the last days, in the tribulation, if there would be a tribulation, or before the tribulation, when Christians and Jews are once again persecuted, as they are persecuted now in other countries. I tried not to be concerned with such thoughts, but in that Scripture, I saw a little dark alley of time in which terrible things happen. Often, in the past, I refused to listen to Frank and his uncle argue over translation. My husband wanted to make another attempt at translating the Bible. It seemed his uncle John wanted to work with him.

Thankfully, I had a call from Winnie. I was on the phone listening to the glories of museums and restaurants during her visit with Helen. Thankfully, it took her a while to tell me everything they had done. But when she finished, I returned to Frank and Uncle John's conversation as though I had not been gone from it.

"'Go your way till the end; for you will rest and stand in your place at the end of the days' (Dan 12:13)."

Often, it seemed to me that their journey into words was like my journey into the formation of clay. I was always aware that it was earth I was working with in my ziggurats, while Frank formed, or tried to form, some understanding of heaven.

Thelma, John's wife and Frank's aunt, made her husband happy. I wondered how she did it. Often she came with him and sat knitting as they talked. She had nothing in her way, like I did.

I only wanted to be alone in my work shed with my ziggurats. Aloneness is a grace in which the world alone reveals its aloneness. By grace, I received singleness, though I have been married to my old companion, Frank, for years and years. I formed that understanding, or that search for understanding, in my clay ziggurats here in my work shed.

Sometimes, someone was there who knew me, who stood aside. Whoever it was, they were filled with grace. Those places of grace were close together, like stepping-stones, but they were almost too far apart. I couldn't step from stone to stone with grace, but an awkwardness was always there for me.

Was that in the days after my collapse? Or was it the later confusion when the past would come as though it were the present?

Singleness was a place called Nazareth—small and out of the way. A sidelight on a tour. Not important as other places.

I worried about my son Warren's aloneness. Had being in a troubled family frightened him away from having a family of his own?

God kept his way hidden (Isa 45:15). Frank used that verse several times after Daniel's death. God's way was in the unacceptable death of Daniel, and in the unacceptable death of Christ on the cross. Couldn't there have been another way?

There was a loneliness that came with marriage. I can't say which I liked least.

At Its Deadliest

OFTEN, I HEARD FRANK making grunting sounds, as if each breath took an effort. As if it was a chore, a strain. I wanted to put him out of his misery. I think I knew, eventually, we'd put him in a grave beside Daniel in the Winscott family plot in the cemetery north of Fenton.

I began to notice he could not work as he used to. He would tire by afternoon. In the evening, he could not even read.

Then I found him asleep in his chair.

"Are you in pain?" I asked, pushing the mop of hair from his forehead. "Do you hurt anywhere?"

"No," he said. He did not. He was just weary of study. It interested him, but he couldn't hold to it. He would have to wait until morning. I think he worked at night in his sleep. I could feel him reading beside me. That's what dreams must be. Journeys we map for ourselves. Or maybe it's a journey the dreams map for us. At least a portion of them, anyway. But then, in the darkest night, something else happened. The subconscious took over and became the engine room. Often I woke with an idea about another ziggurat, thinking how to form the flames in a different way. There were many levels to sleep. I was glad of my tiredness at night.

I worried about Frank and me from time to time. I hoped that we would remain absorbed by our own attitudes and foolishnesses until there was nothing left of us. I hoped that we wouldn't have that long waiting period to die, but that we would simply vanish at the end of our work.

I thought of my ziggurats as I peeled potatoes of an evening—they seemed terraces for a ziggurat. As I stirred the pan, I made concentric circles.

> Journal entry, August 21: *How hard to tell what a wild, rough, and stubborn wood it was.*
>
> —Dante, *The Divine Comedy*, canto 1

What happened to the children that used to run through the house? Where was the group of friends that gathered on the sofa and chairs on Sunday evenings to talk about *The Divine Comedy*? Maybe Frank and I had to work to forget it all.

My husband could spend the morning in his study with the smell of old books. His bookshelves covered the walls from floor to ceiling. If he had a new book, it soon absorbed the smell of the old. What was language? How many ways were there to say what he wanted to say? How could Scripture be interpreted? Over and over, until the language changed its meaning in a subtle way that was hardly noticeable until it was too late. Or if one sentence changed but another did not, a new way had to be configured to read their relationship to one another.

Why did we even need language to say what was needed? Meaning seemed to be in the image. The seen object. The object seen. The impact of the visual. Say, ziggurats, for instance.

I heard Frank and Uncle John Winscott arguing over some Biblical passage. I hadn't even realized John had arrived. He seemed to appear like one of those mushrooms that came up unexpectedly on the lawn.

"Do you know what that means if you change one word—subvert it so that you don't notice it at first? Can't really, because your mind gives you what you think it should. That's the enemy," Frank said to John. "Not language. Not separate words. But the overall engine that gauges it. That weighs it. That subverts it. That is the master cylinder. The master changer. The human mind that is full of tricks. A magician."

Well, it was better than the sad life of a traveling clown.

Often on Sunday we made it to church. Frank in the front row, always leaning forward. I was afraid he'd levitate to the pulpit. John, also a retired minister, was poised to follow.

Often, Uncle John and Thelma came to our house after church for supper. After the meal, we left the men to themselves. We shared e-mails from our children and walked through the leaves in the yard down the drive to the road.

At Its Deadliest

———•◆•———

"Should we go for a walk?" Frank sometimes asked. Should we drive to Fenton? Should we go to the store? Should we find a shore where we can collect shells? Should we try to live again? The answer was always no. We would rather work. A new ziggurat was coming. Another possibility for translation. We couldn't be caught away from our desk and the table in the work shed. It was too risky. We might not be able to reconnect if we were gone too long. But we took risks each day with our work. We were made of risk. It was always inside our work shed and study, where the possibility could exercise itself. That was the main ingredient—the proximity to where the risk could unrisk itself.

Frank loved translation. English into English. That was no small task.

Language is wobbly at best. Because meaning rides upon it—communication and understanding—which is survival. It is absolutely devastating at worst. It can turn upside down. It can sit crosswise in the stream. It can confuse. Subvert. It's a game of interpretation. At its deadliest, it is war.

Sparses

ONCE, WE DECIDED TO have supper alfresco. In those days, it was still acceptable to use the fire pit in the backyard. We wrapped our potato and carrots and meat in tinfoil and baked them in the open fire. As we ate, I heard Daniel howl. In the dark, he was eating the tinfoil around his potato, which sent a jagged pain from the fillings in his teeth into his head. Warren and Winnie laughed. Frank gave Daniel a frigid lecture on how to unwrap the foil from a baked potato before eating. Daniel, in tears, ran to his room and stayed under the bed until sometime in the night.

Sometimes I woke from a nap with memories pasted to me. I made note of them to work into my ziggurats. The smell of burning leaves in the fall. The smell of woodsmoke from a house somewhere on the hill. The memory of summer heat. The museum of winter cold.

In grade school, girls wore dresses that barely covered the knees. In winter, it was a time of continually being cold. There were leggings when I played in the snow, which often became frozen rain. Maybe the houses were not well insulated. Or there were little spots of warmth from the furnace around which great spurts of cold prevailed.

Language becomes chapped with the cold. It is an image of restoration. Not restoration itself. A something to get at something else. A something that has to be used to get at something else that cannot be gotten at otherwise.

"A subversion of desire, a thwarting—a sublimation like marks I made in the sand, erased as soon as they were made," Frank said to someone, maybe himself.

"'Surrogation' is another word that comes to mind, if it is a word," I said.

Frank and his uncle John Winscott used to argue. Thelma, his wife, and I would stand on the porch until they finished, the children playing in the field or by the creek—Daniel, Warren, Winnie, John II, Lizbet, and Thomas.

John was only several years older than Frank. They were more like brothers. Thelma was younger, nearly my age.

"There's a vacilation of language, and in its wobbliness, a direction of meaning of the highest order can survive," we heard Frank say.

"Between the cherubim, I suppose," John added.

"It's abstraction that allows the other to be acknowledged, if not captured," I heard Frank say. "There is little capturing in language. You go on a hunt. You may hunt all morning, and again in the afternoon, but the catch eludes you. You may hunt while sleeping. What is dreaming but a hunt?"

"That's what I want to do," I said to Thelma as we made a casserole for supper. "I want to hunt for the connectives there also. Mainly the land, which I feel when I play with the children in the clay. That's why I like to travel to places. I get ideas," I said. "But I don't like graveyards. I don't visit Civil War cemeteries. I remember being in England, visiting the graves of the American war dead, then leaving with a heaviness and sadness that stayed with me the rest of the trip. I felt their longing for life. Their grieving that they didn't have a chance to live—maybe still carrying the pain, the maiming, the brokenness, the fear of battle with them. The tour guide asked if I was all right as the bus left. I told her I could feel their longings, and she looked at me with suspicion the rest of the trip." I looked at Thelma, but she was staring at the potatoes as she peeled.

"Maybe it was the feelings of the families the soldiers left behind that you felt," Thelma said, still not looking at me.

Often, I felt Thelma didn't understand what I said. I thought she thought I was weird but kept it to herself. I felt I could say anything, and she would not grasp it. It would pass through her and be forgotten. But there were other times when I knew she understood my words.

A smear is what language is. A sparseness. A sparses. It takes the invention of words. It's what a ziggurat is. The essence of getting at the abstraction. An aptitude for making what doesn't exist until you make it. It is an indirect method of talking about—a talking about talking. A presentation of something like what it was like, but that cannot be reached because there are no connectives there. Or there is something that has no body. No physical presence. It is known by its effect on something else. The way the wind scatters the leaves.

We were corralling children then, calling them to supper.

"Don't grieve over language," I said to Frank at the table, "just because meaning rides upon it." Why did I give Frank a hard time? I should set him loose from my sarcasm. I remember the children looking at me.

Frank worked all day with words, but never could quite tell me in words what he thought. But I could tell by his dejected mood that language was stalking him again. I slowly realized he was the hunted, not the hunter.

There were nights when I felt I heard the crunching of bones. Something had Frank in its teeth. Sometimes I knew there was no night, only continual struggle.

We went to the doctor in Fenton for Frank's tiredness. He was given a prescription. When we left the pharmacy, I saw a man crossing the street. He looked at us as he passed, then looked away quickly as I turned to watch him. I knew in an instant that he had known Daniel. He was somehow connected. I looked at Frank. I wanted to say, "Let's follow him. Let's find out what he knows about what happened to Daniel." Frank looked at me with disturbance. I didn't want to cause further turmoil for him. The living were more important than the dead.

I looked for the man, but I didn't see him again. In my mind, I had seen Daniel's supplier. I think he was in the cemetery at Daniel's funeral. I couldn't be sure, but I had a vague memory of someone standing off to the side of the crowd. How many undercurrents were there? How many spidery tendrils to our events?

Frank woke dizzy sometimes in the morning, like he'd been whirling in sleep, and it took a while for him to get his grounding back. I wondered at times if he'd been in search of Daniel.

"And where is Frank?" the women asked at a town meeting in Fenton. Their husbands didn't inquire.

"He's translating."

"What is he translating?"

"The Bible."

"I thought it had been translated."

"Certain parts of it have," I said.

"The whole thing, I believe," one of the women commented.

"Yes, the words have been translated. But he works with the meaning of those words. What they really say, underneath. Translation is difficult at best. An impossibility at its worst." I wanted to leave these women in my wake. I'd known them for years, and we had never connected. "I hear Frank groan from the other room when I am fixing supper." I took them into my confidence. They listened intently. "I think how fortunate it is that our roles are not reversed. I can think about meals or folding laundry. I asked him once to fold the towels, thinking it would relieve him of some of his burden of translation, but it sent him into another conundrum. He saw himself folding pages of language over and over."

The women looked at me, most of them puzzled as to the point.

"You'd think he would want to get away from it now and then," one of the women said.

"If he finishes, he will be here."

"The whole Bible, you say?"

"No, the portion he's working on," I tried to explain to the women. "Frank's working with how words fold into one another. He thinks about it for days. The absorption of words. But it's him they absorb more than one another."

The women wanted Frank to be there to entertain them with his thoughts. "The Bible is a trampoline from which various jumps can be made." That was one of his statements. They would look at one another, wondering what he would say next. I think how an abstract can be framed in a narrative—that was another one of his remarks.

"It's like the impossibility of carrying water in a cattle truck—sloshing all around, spilling over the road, an annoyance to anyone who follows. Maybe a danger," I said. "He works with the nonrepresentational. That is the thrill of it. Sometimes he finishes a translation session with a statement."

"What kind of statement?" the women asked.

"'Let them praise your name, for it is holy.' That kind of statement."

Frank's Uncle John was a translator in his own right. He also had been a minister. Whenever I was in the house, I listened as he and Frank discussed the Bible.

Often, he jumped here and there, not staying on the subject at hand. He was a man in his late seventies. Thelma had not come with John that evening. She had to stay with her children, or maybe it was her grandchildren. Time had a way of wobbling back and forth over itself.

My rebellion was marrying a religious man. Becoming an indirect Christian, an unintentional Christian by an intentional act, but I hadn't realized I would end up in church all the time. That was back when the relatives were alive. Frank and John's family filled John's mother's house on Thanksgiving. Frank and I, John and Thelma, had not replicated ourselves the way they had. Our children seemed to replicate themselves even less. There was no drawing power in our houses. I felt that Warren and Winnie returned to the emptiness of their former house until it was time to return to their lives. Thelma said she felt the same, though I knew her children were home more often than mine. As glad as I was to see my children, why did we feel an awkwardness when they came?

"'For the law having a shadow of good things to come, and not the very image of the things, can never with those sacrifices which they offered year by year continually make the comers thereunto perfect' (Heb 10:1)," Frank said.

Frank and his uncle John would discuss the shadows in that passage for the morning. Arguing sometimes. Once, from my work shed, I heard Frank's voice and went to the house. John Winscott was frail, though energetic. When he first stood after sitting a while, he steadied himself with his hand on the back of the chair. I found him standing that way when I entered the house. I don't think Frank realized how overbearing he was when he was set on making a point. I calmed him with cranberry bread and tea. John sat down again.

"It is not possible that the blood of bulls and goats could take away sin," Frank tried to continue until I hushed him. "'He takes away the first that he could fulfill the second' (Heb 10:9)." Frank made one more attempt, until I glared at him.

They were into similitudes and shadows and the realities toward which the similitudes pointed. It was right up my alley. It was my work in clay.

I tried to subvert my ziggurats. I tried to give them my shadows. I work blending colors. Frank works blending words. We both work with nuance. Hue. Shade. I know it's the same with words. Frank works with shadings of words. I work with the sound of clay.

"Don't put more on yourself than what you're able to achieve," Frank said.

"I'll keep your words in mind."

Uncle John Winscott went home that night exhausted. I tried to get him to stay, to sleep in Warren's old room, but he refused.

"Thelma would be all right for one night," I insisted, but he wouldn't listen.

I got the feeling he felt he was fleeing our war, small as it was. "Skirmish" was the better word.

But John Winscott apparently cared for neither.

"Do we have to go to church again?" I asked on Sunday morning.

"I'm a minister," Frank answered. "Let us not forsake 'the assembling of ourselves together' (Heb 10:25)."

Was that the irony? After all our efforts. We were sheep that clung together lest we see the ridiculous gospel we followed? Lest we know we belonged to a religion in which we could do nothing but believe? The high rate of intelligence seen in some, the achievements, the accumulation of honors and efforts, meant nothing? What a joke God played on us. How against human instinct. They counted me as one of them, so I didn't have to examine my standing in the faith. I didn't have to look at faith. It failed my hearing daily.

We backed our old car from its shed and turned around in the yard to start down the drive. I noticed some old tire ruts beside the drive, which a recent mowing had uncovered.

As I listened to the sermon in church, I had to keep up with the Bible to give Frank a hard time.

"How much sorer punishment who has trodden under foot the Son of God, and has counted the blood of the covenant wherewith he was sanctified an unholy thing" (Heb 10:29). How sobering. God was the one in charge. Our world was a sheep pasture from which he chose his flock. No, no that couldn't be. I drove my ladder into the ziggurat of hell.

Once there, my core was shaken. Like the Russian mathematician who proved the universe was oval and could not work in mathematics again. I can't remember his name, but he had flown above the gravity that holds us in our dimness for a purpose, and he couldn't return.

"Grigori Perelman," Frank said later.

Several Nights after Daniel Died

SOMETIMES IT CAME BACK all over again, floating like an island through the sea of our years.

The police had trouble rousing us. I heard the knocking long before I realized what it was, and that I had to do something about it. I knew Frank could not be roused. It was up to me. I couldn't remember if Winnie and Warren had left to start out on their own, or if maybe one of them wanted back in, maybe forgetting their keys. Daniel had not come around in a while, and my first dread was that it was him.

We had gone to bed early, as we always did. When I could sit up in bed, I looked at the clock. It was 10:30 pm. It was hardest to wake when I'd only been asleep for a couple of hours. If it was later in the night, it would have been easier.

I sat up and fumbled with the covers. The room was unfamiliar in its darkness. Frank's clothes rested in a chair. Shoes were scattered on the floor. Shadows from the hall light made a path from the bed. I found my robe and crept down the stairs, holding onto the railing so I wouldn't fall. I realized the knob on the bannister was still loose, though Frank said he had tightened it.

I turned on the front light and opened the door. Two policemen were there.

"The headlights of a passing car struck metal on a curve north of Fenton," they said. Daniel had been found. He had been dead several days. Whose car? I asked. Someone they didn't know. It had been stolen. Could we identify the body?

I told the officers it was impossible to wake my husband once he was asleep. He'd had a long day of translating, and I remember him being overly tired at supper.

Several Nights after Daniel Died

One of the officers went with me into the kitchen and sat with me at the table. The other officer went upstairs to wake Frank. I realized how cluttered and overgrown the kitchen seemed as I saw the officer's eyes go over the room.

———•·•———

At the morgue, I saw Frank talking to one of the officers. It was decided that only Frank would see the body. I would have to wait for him to return. I protested, but an officer said he would wait with me.

Frank returned, ashen faced. He told me the body was Daniel.

———•·•———

Daniel was dead. Daniel was dead. All the frustration. All the anger. The fear. The buzzing I always heard from the engine that ran the world. Cruelly. Cruelly. Daniel was the channel. Now, Daniel, our son, was dead. He was our grief. Finally, his death was our relief. After expecting the news for years. After all the shame that still burned. Daniel's thievery. His attempt to accost Helen Harsler. His failures. Daniel was dead. After all my years slapping clay—all my years working with ziggurats, which were my translations in the space between rage and ragged forgiveness. Daniel was dead. Hope and despair were over. Daniel was dead. We would go on now without him. Frank took my arm and pulled me from the chair. I stood beside him as he signed the coroner's paper—and we left the morgue.

We drove home in our separate worlds, each thinking our own thoughts, each wondering what happened to our lives. I slept in Winnie's room that night, as I had done before. For some reason, I didn't want to be with Frank.

What Is There in Ziggurats That Words Cannot Say?

I MADE ZIGGURATS—LIKENESSES OF Dante's nine rings of fire—only my funnel went up, something like the tower of Babel. Nothing you see everyday.

My work shed, when I approached it in the morning, a steaming cup of coffee in my hand, the birds singing my path through the weeds, seemed a ziggurat itself. The roof started to rise, then was capped, or allowed to go unfinished. It actually was an attempt of Frank's to let more light into the shed.

"A roof window," he said.

"But I don't want the light streaming down," I protested. "I want light from the side—through the windows."

Frank, not much of a builder, was unable to finish it anyway.

I couldn't wait until my hands were slick and wet with clay and water. I could feel them in my hands even before I entered the work shed. Was it an old rebellion from having to be clean as a child, not allowed to play in the dirt that called to me?

All day I worked. I was hardly aware of anything except the birds that chirped in the windows—and Frank knocking on the window when he wanted lunch. On the road, there was a sign that pointed the way to my clay works: "Clay figures for sale, mainly ziggurats." It was rare that anyone came. Rarer still that anyone bought my clay forms.

My husband stayed in the house translating the Bible while I was in my work shed.

"You should fix lunch for yourself," I told him when I saw him at the window again.

"It's for you," he said. " Otherwise you wouldn't eat."

Frank talked about his work at lunch, while I talked of my ziggurats. Our conversations rarely crossed the same intersection, unless it was our children—unless it was Daniel. But Daniel was dead. Daniel was dead, I assured myself.

"In time, you'll get over your anger," Frank said.

"I doubt it," I answered.

In my work shed again, a yellow jacket at the screen sounded like a truck on the road in the distance. It had a particular growl as if it were plowing snow. Or maybe it was the mower on a far edge of the field. I looked up to see what season it was. Summer, of course. The summer of storms. Just as the winter had been.

Maybe the growling I heard was from my own throat. I had a bucket of water, a workbench on which to throw and knead the clumps of clay. A water-spotted page on which I calculated the sections for the new piece. What else would it be but a ziggurat?

The stouter ziggurats I made were hollow inside, or they were in sections. Otherwise, they could not be fired because of their thickness. No matter how slowly I fired them, I could not get rid of the water in the clay. In the early days, I had a graveyard for the ziggurats I had to discard. I could see their little humps through the window like small Indian burial mounds. My first kiln ran on house current. Sometimes, I ordered the pugged clay I used through the nearby college. They knew I was a potter. Why hadn't I been asked to teach there? I could have talked about underglaze and my methods of overglaze. I could go back to the shaping of the clay in my hands. Clay becomes more pliable the longer you have it. Potters in China made clay for the next generation. Sometimes I told Frank that clay must have a Christian origin. No matter what I did, the clay was forgiving.

Sometimes I made my own clay, pouring the powdery material into a large bowl, my nose and mouth covered with a face mask, my hands and clothes covered with work gloves and an apron. Sometimes Frank made of list of dangers: borax, cobalt, lead, sulfite. I could have listed a few others.

"Look what you track in the house," he repeated. "Look at your sleeves. I don't want to eat lead for lunch."

In my work shed, I had my jars of brushes with their arms held up. My bottles of mixed colors. The round tubs of my Skutt kilns. The UPS truck arriving in the drive with another hundred-pound sack.

We had a short visit from Warren and a girlfriend. I saw her look of amazement at our place, which could be called overgrown, I suppose. Maybe it was more like horror the morning she came to my work shed to watch me work. It had been expanded from an old tool shed. Maybe she was impressed with the quaintness of it. Maybe she was wondering what held the work shed in place without toppling. I saw her eyeing the sagging shelves and tables covered with clay and dyes of all sorts. She looked at my kilns, my work utensils, the sticks and found objects, my books with their torn pages, my journals with their pages curled up. She stared at my clutter of ziggurats. My aprons covered with clay. The old air conditioner that buzzed like a fruit fly.

"When I first came in, your forms looked like rocks I used to collect. They were standing there all by themselves in their odd shapes. Then I saw they were clay. But they still look like a rock city," she said.

I thanked her for her comment. I hoped Warren liked this girl.

Maybe art was a place where the bones of the dream came through, and I chewed on them a while. Maybe ziggurats were part of a darker world that dreams could only hint at, and I had to look at them a while. Lose a child. Stare at the sun. Watch the moon walk away from you at night. Pick a rock here. A rock there. I could only guess at her misperception. Or was it mine? Why did my art seem more interesting than Frank's world? Unless I could see the Bible as a structure of ziggurats. That was my work—seeing it all in my own way.

Seeing as I chose to see.

A Ziggurat Is a Funeral Umbrella

A BLACK CLOUD COVERED the sky. Arms of rain pummeled the car. The rain pushed across the fields and blew down upon the road. There was hail with the rain, then rain again.

"Frank, we should stop," I said, but he kept driving.

The tossing trees spilled leaves and small branches across the road. The storm splattered us with leaves, detritus, and bits of trash.

"Stop, Frank," I battered. "Stop now." Lightning flashed. The windshield wipers pounded back and forth.

Frank was in a trance, staring at the road ahead, his hands grip-locked on the steering wheel.

Oncoming cars pulled off the road.

He had the caution lights flagging everything out of our way, as if oncoming cars should get off the road so we could pass, as if the leaves had eyes and ears so they would know not to splatter our car. It was nearly dark as night, though midafternoon by the clock.

Frank plowed on at his usual ten miles an hour. It was as though the cars got off the road to make space for us to pass in the corridor of the storm.

Just think if this were snow.

Rain continued to flog the car. We'd been at the grocer's in Fenton when the storm started and were returning to our place. Though I asked Frank to stay in town until the storm passed, or the worst of it, he wouldn't listen. The smell of rain was pungent. It actually was the smell of dust that had been in the air I smelled. The rain was bringing it down. It was laundry day in the sky. The battering wind was the sheets hanging up. It was also the smell of the dirt-clotted potatoes in the damp brown paper sack we had purchased—blue potatoes. Dirt from the air and dirt from the earth reunited. It was also our own smell of fear at the moment. My work apron in the backseat because I'd worn it to the grocer's before Frank reminded me to take it off. Or maybe the smell was our determination as we beat our way through the storm, the smell of rain and dirt bringing back the funeral of our son, Daniel, which took place during a lingering squall leftover from a hurricane in the gulf. All the funeral guests stood clumped together clutching their umbrellas.

Why was someone given if he would be taken? Why would I understand, then forget what I thought I had understood? My child Daniel's death. Our adult child, his mind mangled by drug use.

Ziggurats Are the Figmentor of Imagination

SHE WAS A BLUE woman—the dreams that delivered ideas for my ziggurats—as if a supply train had made it through the dark to the front line. She was an idea, or instinct, or the need to form or misform the clay in my hands. Maybe she was like the man Daniel saw by the river in the book Frank always was quoting. There was a unity between us. A relationship. I was complete when I worked with clay. It was more than clay. I was connected with something outside myself. Or maybe the blue woman was within. She was hard to describe. It took a ziggurat to do so. And me trying to wake in the night when I had an idea, fumbling for the notebook I kept on a table beside the bed, knocking over flashlight, bifocals, pencil, a low glass of water.

Catfish blue—the idea I woke with that morning as I continued to work through the blues with my ziggurats. What would blue look like if it were shaped? That was a question the blue woman had asked in my sleep. As if sleep itself were one of the railcars on the supply train.

Blue horse. Blue dog. Blue boy when he was gone.

A ziggurat is a finger pointed at God's driveway. He has a lot to answer for, I think in my angry moments, which last most of the day.

Sometimes I stopped work when I heard the mail truck at our box. The brakes had a particular squeak I heard even in my deepest concentration. I still expected a letter from Warren. A postcard from Winnie. An explosion from Daniel.

My son, Daniel, died in misery. Physical pain, of course, but the isolation as he faced the sky.

Wisteria. Hyacinth. Dahlia. Prussian blue. Garter blue. Italian blue. Dresden blue. Madder blue. Devils with a blue back. And of course, the devastation of blue ruin. It may have been a blue jacket instead of yellow at the window, whining with noises I couldn't explain.

Maybe it was Daniel's infant voice as I held him, rocked him, tried to quiet him. There had been a distress in him from the beginning. Winnie and Warren, our other children, never had it. They were restless at times, belligerent in their adolescence, but Daniel's disturbance at the core was not in them.

I read the book of Daniel after Frank had named our firstborn. I found the passage "we are found wanting" in Dan 5:27 in the stale, yellowed pages of my childhood Bible. Maybe that was our Daniel's heart. I read a further passage, "I saw one like a human being coming with the clouds of heaven" (Dan 7:13). Maybe that's where he reached when he wrecked.

Daniel crossed the blue edge of a hill in the middle of a summer's night. He went over the embankment. No one saw what happened or found him until too late. There, in his stupor, injured, unable to move, his neck broken, his body twisted in a backward way, he lived for several hours, the coroner said. His cries are the blue hornets that still circle the ziggurats in my work shed. The circling cries shape the clay in my hands. For Daniel, they were a way out of this life that could not be lived. Who first sold him? Who first gave him his way to death? Why could no manner of restoration take him?

Camel. Stork with blue feet. Goat. Sheep. The dream of Daniel in his head on his bed. Lion. Bear. Leopard. An unnamed beast with iron teeth and a round, blue tongue—let it be called addiction.

I saw the Ancient of Days on his throne in a blue garment because he wore the sky for a coat. "One like the Son of man came with the clouds of heaven, and came to the Ancient of days, and they brought him near before him. And there was given him dominion and glory" (Dan 7:13–14).

"It is our assurance," Frank said. "We are spared."

"Then why does it feel like we're not?" I asked him.

Beasts with teeth of iron tried to tear Daniel from the car, ripping his flesh for several days. No one knew where he was or where he had been going. Frank would not let me see him. But I saw Frank toss in his sleep for nights afterwards. As if the same beasts were pulling him from our bed.

My blue period followed. No, it began the first time I knew Daniel flew high. I made my ziggurats to reach him. But he flew higher over the top of any ziggurat I could make. It was in the pupils of his eyes—those black holes—those large pits into which he fell—those swarming visions Frank muddled over in the Bible.

It's been three years. Maybe four. Maybe thirteen. Maybe fourteen. It was a long time ago. It just happened.

I still make my blue ziggurats, trying to follow Daniel. To call him back. Me and the insects circling my shed.

It was Daniel who called out to the bright shades of clay in the hobby section in back of the hardware store in Fenton when he was a boy. It was me who first bought the clay and formed shapes with the children. They moved on to other interests. I kept working with the clay.

In the first year after Daniel's death, Frank spent time going over papers and more papers. We were sued by the owners of the car Daniel had wrecked. We were sued by people to whom Daniel owed money. Daniel, of course, had no insurance. We received other letters saying Daniel was in debt to them, but many of Daniel's transactions were not legal, and they had no ground to stand on. We hired a lawyer in Fenton to close Daniel's affairs.

If I Start to Nap, I Growl

After lunch each day, I returned to my work shed, passing our car, which Frank had left in the drive, still stuck with leaves from the storm we passed from Fenton. The birds were quieter in early afternoon.

I formed clay in a spiral, cutting it into parts with the ulu I bought from a Yup'ik on a trip to Alaska—a cutting knife curved like a quarter moon. As though the ziggurat were deer meat. Moose meat. I couldn't remember why we were in Alaska. It was long ago. Maybe Frank visited missions there, and we left our children with Uncle John and Thelma Winscott, just as they left their children with us sometimes when they traveled.

I, Eugena, kept journals that sat on the shelf. Sometimes I heard the voices of ziggurats as I worked with them. I wanted to make note of what they said. Sometimes I heard their voices before they were made. They spoke in small clumps of thought, or fragments. Sometimes they made buzzing sounds like a yellow jacket at the screen or a motorcycle in the distance.

I thought of Frank in the house, going over his papers. He had a sound mind—the kind that liked study. But he had to keep the focus of his study moving. In that we were alike. Nothing was unexamined. He had a fundamental mind that reached for a fundamental understanding of the subject he was studying. But his study was about Biblical passages. Or commentary on Biblical passages. Or consideration of Biblical passages in relationship to one another. My *research*, on the other hand, was about clay. It headed away from God. Frank's work drove straight into him. But though we worked in our separate places, it was as though we were together.

> Journal entry, July 6: *The ziggurat entered my thoughts when I roasted a duck. Blue-red. Blue-brown. Blue-black.*

Beside my journals, there were other books on the shelf in my work shed: Homer. Thucydides. Lucretius. Tacitus. *The Divine Comedy*. The

History of Herodotus—the incompatibility of man and the world in which he lived. What else is new since fifth-century Greece? And *Ziggurats and Me*, which are my journals. The shelf was swaying in the middle—I would have to ask Frank to nail up another support under it.

July as blue. Though we have two other children, the loss of Daniel is a ziggurat before me. I climb the steps up and up, as if ascending the crumbling wall of China. Blue as Van Gogh's bedroom in his painting. Chopped as Picasso's portraits. Musty as the Holy Land.

She was a blue woman. She came at night. Packed with ziggurats. She made them in her head and gave them to me to work out with my hands and the craziness of my anguish. The act of creation is like that. Ziggurats. Their abstractions. Their underlying meanings. They blazed while I struggled for ordinary thoughts—while I e-mailed Warren and Winnie, while I had a normal conversation with Thelma on the phone, while the women of Fenton called for another meeting on what kind of banners to fly at town events, or what flowers to plant in the town flowerpots for spring, summer, and fall seasons. I had ignored most of their invitations, as I had ignored Thelma when she didn't want Daniel in her house anymore. I thought it was her fault—whatever little skirmishes there had been. I even ignored the fact that she didn't ask us to watch John II, Thomas, and Lizbet again.

I was a maker of ziggurats. Blue ziggurats. Cerulean. Teal. Gentian. Azure. Indigo. Watchet. Mazarine. Arctic blue. Pontoon blue. The blue I made by twisting different clays and blue dyes. Mixing them, not keeping notes in my journal so I could re-create them. God was a re-creator. Did not the world exist before it was void? Did not God start again? Are there not two stories of creation in Gen 1 and 2?

I thought of blueing. I thought of blue eye from a disease in which the iris was erased—no, that was milk eye, wasn't it? I thought of the difficulty of arranging one's eye to see the mixes in nature.

I was the slave of ziggurats. As Daniel in Babylon had been. Hadn't he been an outcast of sorts? As our Daniel in Fenton had become.

Sometimes a ziggurat is a pointed hat for the earth. A dunce in the corner of the universe.

Often on the hill, the clouds are a corkscrew staircase into the air—a ziggurat in the text of rising. An ascension from earth. A wicked will asking to pilot its own way. That's what I asked. So no God would take my son. Self was more trustworthy than God.

It was raining in my head. Weather. Weather. Whether inside or out. One storm after another.

A ziggurat is a manual of war. It maneuvers through storms. On the battlefield of the work shed, ziggurats vie for position. The work shed loves battle.

Every time we thought Daniel's affairs were closed, they opened again. The owners of the car said some of the belongings were missing when they searched it in the salvage yard. A cell phone. A charger. A GPS. A briefcase. Tools. A Pendleton blanket. They sent a list. Maybe someone else had stolen the car Daniel wrecked. Maybe someone found the car in the ravine. Who knows what happened? Would Daniel's messes follow us forever? Still others continued to find grounds on which to sue us. Or they tried to sue. Or they sent threatening notes that Daniel owed them money. But it was below board, and there was nothing they could do. Frank gave the notes to the sheriff, but they were not traceable. At night, when I heard a car passing the house, I did not always know if it was a patrol car, or one of Daniel's friends trying to scare us. On several weekends, Warren stayed with us.

Casting Doubt

It comes back to my memory now. The police returned to our house. There was a dent in the back fender of the car Daniel was in when he died. It didn't seem consistent with the wreck. The owners said it wasn't there when the car was taken. Maybe the driver of the tow truck had dented it when he pulled it from the ravine. I thought the investigation had closed.

"Could Daniel have been followed or pushed?" I asked.

"Did Daniel have enemies?" the investigator asked.

"You know he was a drug user," I said. "You've been on his tail a long time. Not to help—not to find out who was supplying him, but to harass."

"Eugena," Frank said.

The officers talked to Frank while I left the room. I was steaming. I sat in Frank's study, listening to their voices from the other room.

I saw Frank's journals open on the floor. His uncollected papers. I kicked them away with my feet.

Daniel had accosted Helen Harsler years ago. I didn't know if it was an attempted rape, or if he was following some bizarre link to her in his irrational mind. Helen never spoke of it to us. Daniel had stalked another woman for a while. Then there was the car that used to stop on the road at the end of our drive. Several times, I stood with my hand shading my eyes from the sun, my apron flapping in the wind, before the car pulled away. Was it a friend or someone looking to make a drug sale? Maybe they wanted to buy. They didn't know where Daniel was. How was I supposed to know? Where was Daniel? Where did he go all those nights he was out of sight?

"Daniel isn't here," I called out once. "Why do you think he's here?" There's nothing at this house for him but his old parents, bewildered at his addiction.

Once, Frank came from the house and pulled me away from the drive.

What Had I Understood?

MY WORK APRON STILL around my neck, I went in to fix supper.

Once, we had grown our own vegetables. During Daniel's illness, and after his death, the garden went to weeds. We visited farmer's markets and the grocer in Fenton.

"'The prophets stopped the mouths of lions' (Heb 11:33–34)," Frank said at supper. "You could at least remove that blasted apron. You're trailing dried clay everywhere."

I looked at the floor. Frank was correct. I untied the apron and took it to the kitchen.

As I sat at the table again, I looked at him, impatient that he could not leave the Bible. Though he retired from the ministry, he was still at it each day.

I changed the subject. "Where was Daniel going on that remote road?"

"We've gone over that too many times," Frank answered.

"At his funeral, I listened to the rain on the tent," I said. "There was a pattern to it. A rhythm. I wish I knew Morse code."

"Cut it out, Euge," Frank said. "There's no communication from the dead."

"But there is. You read me a passage of Saul who contacted the prophet Samuel when he was dead."

For supper, I ate the memories of Daniel's demands for money. His ugliness to us when we no longer provided him with the means to buy his drugs. His poundings when we locked the door to him and told his brother and sister to do the same. The self. Only the self, where he lived. It was his world of his own self. That was what hell was, Frank said, and I screamed at him to cut the biblical cord of the Bible. To leave me out of his efforts to redeem a scriptural understanding from what had happened.

"It's a chore to believe," Frank said. "The Bible turns away those who would enter on their own terms. That's the story of Cain. He tried

What Had I Understood?

to approach God with the offering he thought he should bring and was rejected. In his anger, he killed his brother. The Lord turned him out, and he became a fugitive and a wanderer."

I took our plates from the table and returned with two bowls of bread pudding.

Frank continued, "'My punishment is greater than I can bear' (Gen 4:13 KJV). I am driven out of the face of the earth. And from your face. Whoever finds me will slay me. Therefore, the Lord set a mark on Cain, lest anyone should kill him. In the NRSV, Cain says, 'I am driven from the soil.'"

"I don't hear the difference," I said with resignation. But that was Frank's work—differentiating between versions of the Bible, translating between the nuances.

In my sleep that night, the blue woman marked my ziggurats on their heads.

The Spiral of the Galaxy—the Spiral of My Ziggurats

"I WANT TO GO over it again," I said to Frank at breakfast the next morning. "There's something buried there, bothering me."

"What are the possibilities, Eugena?" Frank said wearily. "Daniel was lost. No one knew what he was doing on that road. He went to sleep while driving. A patch of the road was slick from rain. He was on his way to a dealer we didn't know. He purposely drove off the road to end his misery. He simply had an accident that was no one's fault, not even his own."

"I think he was so drugged he didn't know he was," I said. "Or I think he had drug-hunger searing his skull. He was following it. Maybe Daniel looked up and saw the lion with eagle's wings. The bear with three ribs in its mouth between its teeth—though the NRSV calls them tusks. The leopard with four wings of a fowl on its back and four heads."

"You've been reading the Bible," Frank said.

"I've seen your notes on the table."

In my work shed, I made notes in my journal:

> Journal entry, October 28: *The spiral of the galaxy in the spiral of a nautilus shell. The spiral of a thumbprint in the spiral of a starch grain that coiled like a flattened ziggurat.*

I remembered Warren's science project using starch grains, which he put under a microscope. They looked like the puddles—the way hills looked like puddles on a contour map. I wished I had spent more time with Warren, but it was Daniel who sucked up all our concern. The condolence notes and sympathy cards still filled the basket on the stubby-legged side-chest in the hall.

At lunch, Frank continued once again, "'I, Daniel, was grieved in my spirit in the midst of my body, and the visions of my head troubled me' (Dan 7:15 KJV). 'As for me, Daniel, my spirit was troubled within me, and the visions of my head terrified me' (Dan 7:15 NRSV). See how those vary?" Frank asked. "'Grieved in one's spirit' is different than 'my spirit is troubled.' 'My spirit in the midst of my body' is different than 'the spirit within me.' It could be anywhere in the NRSV: on top of one's head, under a toenail. But in the KJV, it's right there in the middle of the body. Central to it, in other words. Then there's 'the visions of my head that troubled me,' and 'the visions of my head that terrified me.' The meaning always is somewhere between."

"You're bi-marginal," I said to Frank. "You work in the spaces on both sides."

"Our Daniel is in another world," Frank took my hand. "His tears are wiped away. I don't think he gets another chance at life. I don't think he's sending any messages. Do you know when the devil is talking to you?" Frank asked.

"Yes," I answered. "When I think I can figure it out on my own."

"I want to find the road where Daniel died," I said to Frank one morning.

"No."

"Yes, Frank. It would help," I argued. "Edwin Harsler could drive us. He drives all over the country. I'm sure he's found the place."

"No, he hasn't," Frank said. "I asked him not to go."

"How did he know where it was?"

"The police gave me the general location—several years ago."

"When were you going to share that with me?"

"The weather's unpredictable. Wait until spring."

> Journal entry, November 30: *I saw Daniel calling out to the bright shades of the universe. In his addiction, in that sink hole that pulled drugs into it, that ziggurat at the base of his skull that reached into the unknown, was all the hunger that gnawed him constantly, that gnawed at the world full of addiction.*

Ironic Witness

In my work shed that day, I formed a ziggurat of fire-blue clay. I placed red specks upon it, and russet specks. I placed a small yellow mouth, crooked as a streak of lightning in a storm.

The historian Herodotus said that a shrine was on top of a ziggurat. But I interpreted shrines in my own way. I made long, slender ziggurats with rabbit ears. I made squat pumpkin ziggurats. I made terraced, storied boxes with ramps and spiraled turnings and aerials and satellite dishes. I made ziggurats with handles so God could pick them up. Once men had made ziggurats because God did not get the heavens alone. They tried to form a unit, climb to heaven, keep from being scattered. But that's exactly what happened. How long after their language was confounded did they stay together before it was no use? I made ziggurats with oars and stilts. I made a ziggurat with the iron wheels of a war train. I made a ziggurat covered with armor. I made a ziggurat covered with spikes. I made a ziggurat with a zigzagged boat ramp in ultraviolet. I made ziggurats pounding on my worktable with tears.

By afternoon, the fire-blue ziggurat had horns and wings and I could hardly hold it on the table. I heated the kiln hot as a cremation oven. The air in the work shed buzzed with the prophecies of ziggurats.

In my work shed, my mouth was full of the praises of clay—

Bless the Lord of the work shed.
Bless the Lord of the blue rain slick as the curve on a steep road.
Bless the rhythms and patterns of rain.
Bless the Lord of the blue flame.
Bless the Lord of blue potatoes in their little graves in the ground.

As I woke the next morning, I had a vision of termites. Termite mounds in Australia—I'd seen them on a trip years ago, maybe nearly thirty now. What had brought them back? Frank had gone there for a conference when

The Spiral of the Galaxy—The Spiral of My Ziggurats

he was still in academia. Wasn't it them—the termite mounds—that looked like ziggurats?

Uncle John Winscott arrived soon after breakfast to work with Frank on his translations.

In my work shed, I knew I returned to the termites. I knew I had dreamed of them. And I knew the scaffolding on which I stood was wood. Maybe it was a leftover from the last days of Daniel, when I felt the ground eroding under us. Frank held up his banner of faith through it all, but I knew he was shaken as I was shaken.

"'Though faith we understand that the worlds were framed by the word of God' (Heb 11:3)," John prayed at lunch.

"What worlds?" I asked at lunch, knowing it would get Frank and his uncle John started.

I wanted time to think of Warren's failure to marry his girlfriend, which we had just discovered as I read the e-mail Frank showed me. I knew the breakup would happen. He hadn't mentioned her in a while. What did it feel like to be rejected? The man usually did the asking. It left him open to refusal.

"Are there separate worlds here with us? Is he talking about the different civilizations?" I listened to Frank and John again.

"Who?" Frank asked.

"Paul. Isn't he the author of Hebrews?"

"Yes, I suppose he is," Frank agreed. "That's what biblical scholars say."

"I thought you'd sound more sure, Frank," I admonished him. "You were a professor of biblical studies. You were a minister. Didn't you study this all your life?"

"I want to talk about Daniel again," I said at supper. John Winscott was gone and we were alone. "He was used to our stable world that took us years to accumulate in the ministry and teaching." I saw Frank look at the ceiling. "He was used to our travels and conversations. Your opportunities would not come to him. He dosed himself for consolation. Our life was on a ledge. He couldn't make the jump to it in his own life. It's a different world now."

"It's the same world," Frank argued. "You can't get anywhere when you opt for drugs. Who would hire him? How could he achieve anything? He was unreliable—"

"We stalled at nothing, Frank," I said with rising anger. "Bless God—"

Frank interrupted me with his own anger. "Get off it, Eugena. I'm tired of your excuses for him."

I banged my plate on the table and left the room.

A Freak Snow

FRANK WAS GONE THE day it started snowing, and I worried how he would get back. But the grief I felt that day was not so much from his absence as it was from an isolation or strandedness I did not understand. Somehow, something must have happened long ago when everyone went off together and I was left alone. Maybe it was the aloneness after Daniel passed. Maybe it was an event when everyone received something and I alone did not. I had such a feeling of devastation. It was as if I was abandoned, bypassed, of no notice. Where had it come from? Did my mother leave me alone as a child? Was isolation a punishment I bore as a child and only remembered at times when I had to say goodbye and could not, except with great emotion and tears to the point of incapacity? It had to have been traumatic for me to react all these years later with such devastation.

Maybe it was the sorrow at birth. Of being rejected by the womb. Maybe it was older than birth. Maybe I had to leave a place in heaven to live on this cold earth, for it had always seemed cold to me. In atmosphere more than temperature. Though on days of snow when it came down all day, and the temperature was below zero, and I had walked to class, it actually was cold. There was a separation anxiety in me. It had already happened, and I was reliving it every time I felt isolated or was passed over for articles and awards that went to other workers in ziggurats. Well, to other makers of clay figures. Actually, there weren't many ziggurat makers. I had suffered, somewhere in my life, a very sad parting. I still grieved for it, though I didn't know what it was. It was if an angel had accompanied me to my birth. An angel of which I was extremely fond, and I had to say goodbye and knew I wouldn't see it again, even though it assured me it would be with me. At least until the end of my life, when maybe it would be there again to welcome me back, and I would be agitated and wanting answers as to why we suffered this interminable life anyway. Whose idea was it? I was still in as much of a puzzle as I had been earlier in my life. Maybe more so as the years dragged on.

Frank eventually called and said he would stay with the Canardes overnight, as it was too treacherous to try to come back. Did I have one of my infernal potatoes to peel? Did I have enough in the fridge to make it though the evening and breakfast? Were the tree branches hanging low over the wires? Had I heard a truck plowing the road? Had the lights flickered? Yes. No. Yes. No. I answered all his questions. Did I have any questions? he asked. No. I did not. I would just sit here by myself and count the flakes and chase the squirrels from the birdfeeder and wait for spasms of sorrow to grab my throat.

What mysteries we are to ourselves. I had a warm place on this earth. I was fed. I had my work with ziggurats. I was not alone, other than in my house through a storm. I was not in danger. I lived in peace and safely, except what came from within from the unknown territories of myself. Why did I choose the chute that dropped off into hell? Maybe I didn't believe it was there. It was the wanderers I feared. Only they were without form. They came from within. Memories were their names. The memory of Daniel. I wiped my tears and chided myself for irrational behavior. Just a throwback to something that must have happened once. And if it was so important, why didn't I remember? But having something taken from me that I would have to live without, something that I desperately wanted, or the fact of being away from something or someone I wanted with no chance of retrieval, sent me into a trough of sorrow. I looked from the window at the cruel world and at the disadvantage I had always had, and I felt alone and alone and alone.

Frank called once again in the evening and asked what I was doing. "Sitting by the fire," I said, though there was no fire. "Knitting," though my yarn and needles were in their basket in the other room, as usual. "Reading," I said, though the newspaper had not come, and the books were left closed. I would face the night by myself. I didn't mind, as long as that great sorrow stayed away. Or the mystery of the sorrow. I could understand sorrow at what was real, but not imagined. Maybe I felt this life was a punishment in one form or another, though I didn't believe in reincarnation. I felt we had once to live and once to die. Maybe I could use the isolation I felt as an entryway into the next world. Snowed in. By myself. It seemed a gift, actually. Maybe everything was one long lesson for my ignorance.

I had a call from Winnie later that evening, after she'd seen the news of the storm on television, she said. I told her we were safe.

A Freak Snow

In the night, I thought I heard a lawn mower. Maybe it was the snowplow. I thought I heard creeping in the house. I sat up in bed, my heart pounding. Was Daniel trying to get in the door? Was he was on the mower trying to mow the snow? No, Daniel was dead. If Frank was here, I would think it was his snoring. But I woke enough to remember Frank was gone. I listened to the house for a while, but it was nearly quiet. Maybe the fridge had been having another spasm. Maybe I had dreamed that Edna Woodruff was downstairs with her vacuum cleaner until she too died and pulled away from us. But that would be years later. Maybe it was the jaws of life freeing Daniel from the car he died in, so he could continue to haunt us in our bed.

I listened again. I used reason. The roads had not been cleared. No one would be able to pass along the road. The snow was too deep. I stayed in bed, though I could not sleep. I was angry with memory, which sorted events by its own will, regardless of chronology. I was angry with the craziness that made forays into my thoughts, which I tried to keep straight. No wonder I made ziggurats. They were road markers so I would know the way.

I heard a truck plowing the road in the morning and knew the snow had stopped. It was a neighbor who also came into our drive to push the snow aside with his truck. I waved at him from the front window. Soon I would shovel a path to my work shed, if I could find the old shovel in the garage.

The county was clearing the roads, and everyone would be back to their routines. At least I was not closed in a house with bored and rowdy children. At least I had the privilege of old age when all of that was over. I remember hoping one day it would be over on a day when the children were home from school and had been fussy and mischievous. Discontented and whiney. The children would love playing in the snow, coming in afterwards with red races and puffs of cold rising from their bodies. The times I let go by without putting my finger on them to hold them in place a moment longer. Regret is one of the parts of hell. A minor one—a thorn under the skin of the second finger of the right hand.

Maybe my ziggurats were remembrances of journeys through long days. Upward or downward, depending on circumstances. And what was it I had, after all the struggle through the years? A time to work in my studio pondering ramp ways and similitudes of ramp ways. A place to work at what I willed without interruption. Why was life often weary? Why did

I lose the wonder that was before me when I looked from the window? When I looked at Frank's notes on biblical texts? When I knew, basically, the glory of the Lord who had looked at my sin and voluntarily offered his own body so that I did not have to offer mine involuntarily? I was in old age. I was nearing that passage. I could be lifted from this life at any time. I was already making my way upward on my ziggurats. I just didn't know how far I still had to go.

Frank returned later in the day with a few groceries, apologetic that he hadn't been with me through the storm. The snowplow had passed along the road and into our long drive because Frank paid him to do so. After an early supper, Frank helped me shovel the rest of the narrow path to my work shed.

It turns out he didn't have a pleasant time at the Canardes. There'd been some sort of tension they were working their way through, and they had used him for a buffer zone, passively trying to get him on their side, or to take sides, even though he wasn't sure what the problem was. An affair. A slight. A meanness. A neglect. A recrimination. The usual tension of two people living together for a long time in mutual discontent. What is the burr under the saddle? What is the tension that pulls?

Grounding

OUR HOUSE SAT LOW on the ground. When you came up the road from Fenton, you hardly knew a house was there, though it had two stories and a cupola. Suddenly a roof was visible, then a brown house under it. Frank's study was off the kitchen. The living room had a large fireplace before which two sofas sat. It is where we held our Sunday night meetings on the readings of *The Divine Comedy*. It is where some of my ideas for ziggurats were born.

I remembered one of Frank's prayers, "Forgive our transgressions, Lord," he prayed. "We have broken the Geneva convention. We have broken God's requirements for decent behavior. We have let strangers come into our house. We have not withstood those who would trample us." It's strange how certain parts of the room held the language spoken there. I can look a certain place and remember the words that were said in that particular place. Those latent images we carry. Those mysterious ones within.

When the neighbor's dog became a nuisance, barking at every leaf and whiff of wind in its old age, and they received complaints, they put a bark collar around its neck. When the dog barked and was shocked, it didn't go back to the spot where it barked. It would bark in another place and be shocked, and it would not return to that place either. The dog thought the shock was coming from the place, not the collar. He barked in every corner until he finally had no place to go. I could still see him standing in a back corner of the yard, not moving even whey they called him. It was the shock collar I wore. I knew. I knew.

Downstairs in the house there was a dining room off the kitchen, opposite Frank's study. Over the years, we built a guest bedroom that turned into my work room. Then we built another room, which became my larger work room. Upstairs in our house, our four bedrooms were down a long hall. Outside the kitchen was my dead garden, where vegetables had once stood in their rank and file. My first and second Chronicles, Frank called them, because I had them in order before Daniel's death. "They lodged about the house of God because the charge was upon them" (1 Chron 2:7). There was something about the order, alignment, and chronology of the tribes that once appealed to me.

Finally, we turned a tool shed into my work shed away from the house.

I had been grounded in domesticity as a wife and mother. Shackled. Yet sometimes, outside my chains, I stumbled back into them. I was made for family, even the weariness of it. It was what I knew. Yet I had this wilderness in me—this distant place. It was not the disturbance I felt within. It was a part beyond that part. I used ziggurats to reach it. They were my alternate domesticity. How many places were there for us to discover? How many places did we inhabit as strangers, as immigrants, as pilgrims? We were full of strange places. Unraveling whatever ground we found for ourselves. We are full of ziggurats. They are our attempts to rise on our own.

It's odd how it serves us whole chunks. The way I stir batter and still find unmixed parts. Undissolved. Unresolved lumps.

In a way, I did not keep my eye on domesticity. I had not wanted to know about Daniel's life with drugs. In the beginning, I was suspicious several times, but never convinced until that hard, irrefutable evidence when I saw him high and knew it was a high that was not his first. It had been going on a long time. He was wearing it. He was it.

I felt it long ago—the unthreading into my own end. It wasn't *upward* I was going. I could feel a disturbance within. Were my ziggurats an attempt to climb out of what I saw coming, which was death after life? Or maybe it was life after death that bothered me.

The Prophecies of Ziggurats

AFTER DANIEL'S DEATH, I saw visions in my ziggurats. Frank retreated into his work. Not that he wasn't there already. A retired minister and biblical professor, he worked at translating between different versions of the Bible. An isthmus, he called himself, working mainly between the KJV and the NRSV.

"But you aren't surrounded by water on either side," I said.

"Eugena," he answered with the single word, my name. I could fill in the rest.

My ziggurats didn't speak either, but I knew what they meant. I know what they said just the same. Who needed words to speak? In fact, words often got in the way.

One morning Frank came to the table with his Bible, his hair standing sideways on his head. I knew he had been thinking about Daniel. He read Prov 18:14 to me: "The spirit of a man will sustain his infirmity; but a wounded spirit who can bear?"

I looked at Frank. "What wounded Daniel's spirit?" I asked with anger. "Did he want for anything? Did we hurt him in some way? Did we do anything but love him when he was a child?"

Frank looked at me. "We had to shut him off," he continued. "You realized that before I did." Frank looked at his plate. "An addict would consume the world if he could. There's no end to addiction."

I nodded in agreement. Frank lifted the fork to his mouth, but there was no pleasure in breakfast.

"And exactly what does that passage mean?" I asked. "Does it mean, 'What can a wounded spirit carry?' Or does it mean, 'Who can carry a wounded spirit?'"

"That's why the Bible needs translating," Frank said. "That's why it bears several interpretations. Maybe its spirit is wounded and it puzzles us like Daniel did."

That morning in my work shed, the visions of the ziggurats continued.

Why had I offered Frank words for breakfast? What good did they do? Why did I drive him back into his study? What was he doing there but muddling over Prov 18:14? Reading it again in the KJV. Comparing it to the NRSV. One foot in each version like two rowboats drifting father apart each time he read.

We were going to lose Daniel no matter what we did. We had raised him. He was a man. He made his own decisions. He warped his thinking with drugs until he couldn't see what he was doing. Or if there were moments of clarity when he saw, there was nothing he could do.

What could a wounded spirit bear? Not even the weight of its own wounds.

I worked with the clay that morning, twisting it into a coil that circled upward. I felt the warm anger of it in my hands. It was fresh and taut as the skin of a picked tomato. No—I had a long history of anger at Daniel. That's what I saw in the ziggurat that morning. Just let him move back in one more time. Steal Frank's father's old coins. Our microwave. Bose radio. My mother's silver I had hidden in my work shed. My kilns if he could have lifted them. Just clean up his vomit one more time. Just listen to his tirades and watch the *heebie-jeebies* of withdrawal the times he tried rehab. Just ward off his violence—his unnerving jumpiness—listen in shame for the siren up our road when we called for help. Just listen in court to his terms of probation—and fear for our lives one more night. No, he had to go. We knew that before the counselor told us.

Who can bear a wounded spirit? I thought. It must have eaten Daniel. It must have spit him off the road that night. But we couldn't bear his heavy spirit either.

Unlike Frank, I preferred Proverbs to Psalms. David's words ran over the place with his feelings. Solomon was more in his head. I preferred the visions that occurred as thoughts. I was tired of David's rantings that were too close to my own.

The Prophecies of Ziggurats

I had to sell my ziggurats. They covered my work shed. They covered the house. Every shelf and table. Every cabinet and closet. I even kept some in the barn, though I was afraid it would fall down on them.

I was a maker of ziggurats, those clay figures like the tower of Babel.

I was coming out of my blue phase. I was entering brown. I gave them warning. Who of my ziggurats wanted to hear? The day I woke at zero—facing a landscape like the North Sea. It was all brown, like the sky over it, with the North Sea nowhere in sight.

The nearby town of Fenton had a library. Frank and I visited it. They had two of my ziggurats on display. But there was not room for a showing. There also was a historical museum and a few storefronts in town, but they were crowded with their own wares for the sometimes tourists. There was a bed-and-breakfast that housed a few of my ziggurats on the bureau-dressers in rooms.

Frank and I continued to look for a place to show the small clay figures that covered our shelves. We had talked about opening our tottering barn, but the job of clearing it of rubble was more work than we could handle.

I was changing our sheets one morning when our friend Edwin Harsler stopped by. I saw his truck in the drive from the upstairs window as I pulled the case from Frank's pillow. Frank's hair was wavy. A single hair made a spiral on the case. It looked like a number 6, or a capital G, or the miniature tail of a pig.

"If the ziggurats could be a teapot, or storage jar." I heard Frank say as I came downstairs.

"The story of life," I answered. "If only I could be useful."

"You are useful, Eugena. You've put up with us all these years."

Edwin said a warehouse on Second Street in Fenton had been gutted and turned into an open space of some sort. Upstairs, the owners of the building were trying to sell the rooms for lofts. He had mentioned a showing of my ziggurats to them, which also would welcome everyone to the renovated building.

"As soon as they sweep up the sawdust, you could have a showing of your ziggurats," Edwin offered.

"Let's call it a selling of them," Frank said.

"But who would buy them?" I asked.

"We have friends." Frank said.

"You've lived here all your lives," Edwin suggested.

"You can't give them away, Eugena," Frank said. "You might as well try to sell them. They're bizarre. Even frightening."

"That's what prophecies do."

"What are they prophesying?" Edwin asked.

"Doom, mainly."

"People don't want that in their houses. Life is doomful enough," Frank said. "Make something hopeful. Not those forms with their little pointy heads."

"I like pointy heads, Frank, especially the one sitting on your neck."

I contacted the warehouse—now Fenton's Art and Cultural Center. They agreed to the showing. They wanted me to make a drawing of where I wanted the tables for my ziggurats. The workers would set them up while they were still there. The Figgetts even came to our place one day to see what I meant by my ziggurats. They were puzzled, but they were gracious. They were curious and maybe slightly impressed by my work. Possibly a little horrified.

"They multiply like the lice in Egypt," Frank said.

"Is that what you think of them, Frank?" I asked him later.

"What could I think? You have so many of them. They aren't moving. When was the last time you sold anything? They're crowding us out of the house."

"When did Van Gogh sell anything?"

Edwin Harsler, Frank, and I loaded Edwin's truck with ziggurats and followed him to Fenton's Art and Cultural Center. Notice of the exhibit had been in the papers in several towns, and we expected a crowd. Winnie and Warren thought about coming, but each found they had other commitments. There was a banner in the large plate-glass window. Tea and scones would be served. I wasn't sure any ziggurats would sell. But I would read from my journals. I would talk about the principles of ziggurats. The crowd arrived early. They wandered through the large room full of ziggurats. There

The Prophecies of Ziggurats

was a long slender table up the middle of the room. Ziggurats were lined up on them. I had worried about someone bumping the table and toppling the ziggurats, but the table was walnut, with solid legs and large feet. Heavy as if it were nailed to the floor. It would take more than bump to jar the table, the Figgetts assured me. There also were tables along the walls and shelves above the tables. They were all filled with ziggurats.

There were blue ziggurats that looked ready for battle. Ziggurats with lice in their hair. Ziggurats with water-wings for the crossing of the Red Sea, if it had fallen back into place. Ziggurats with oars for fishing on the Sea of Galilee. Ziggurats swollen as whales. Ziggurats thin as nails. Ziggurats had gone to the cross. Ziggurats spoke for themselves.

It was a chance to visit people you weren't going to invite to your house.

"Eugena," Thelma said, "John and I will man the tables if you want." Crowd control. The Figgetts needed help. Frank's aunt and uncle were willing. Yes, what a crowd. Twenty-five at a time allowed in the room. I had on a new dress with a scarf around my neck. My old one had ripped when I tried it on. At first, I wished I had stayed in my work shed. But I needed to sell my work. Frank and I could use the money. It was my work. My job. It needed to bring in income. It took work to sell. I had to approach people with something other than the sour look Frank told me often was on my face. The ziggurats looked cleaned. Scrubbed. They were on show. They were looked at. Puzzled over. Did I hear a few screaming as they were sold?

I think the people came to see the parents of Daniel Winscott, who had been killed in a car accident or killed himself, after years of reading about his troubles in the newspaper. What had happened? No one knew. But the loss of a child was significant. Especially when connected with addiction. How were we responsible? Nothing I could hear. Nothing I could see. How were we holding up?

At four in the afternoon, the Figgetts called everyone to attention. Chairs were brought in and set between the tables. People took a seat. Others had to stand at the back. They listened to my lecture on ziggurats, their history and significance. Afterwards, they tasked for reason. They asked for theory. Why did I do this? Had I ever thought of making something other than ziggurats? What did they represent? I was a minister's wife. A retired minister. A retired wife? No, I was actively engaged with Frank. He was my husband. We were in love, though the display of love changed over the years. There were more fizzles now, with a few sparks among them.

It was a long question-and-answer session, especially with the careful approach to the subject of our children, Winnie and Warren, and our deceased son, Daniel. I felt open before everyone. I even shared one of Winnie's comments, or maybe it was Warren's: "We have to take a drug test to come home."

There had been storms. But none compared to Daniel's death. An old chicken coup had collapsed. Once, the roof of a garage disappeared into the sky like Enoch in the Bible, leaving the old barn standing. Yes, a garage roof had been translated into the sky, never to be seen again, though a neighbor found a shingle in his petunias that he thought belonged to Frank and returned it. I made a ziggurat blown apart by a storm—with a shingle fragment sticking from it.

They wanted to know more about the ziggurats. I told them what they wanted to know. Every answer they sought with curiosity was embedded in the ziggurats. If they just purchased them—reasonably priced—they would hear their stories.

The exhibit of ziggurats was a visitation more than a sale of ziggurats. No one had known what to say at Daniel's funeral. This meeting was more of a continuation of the visitation, many years later, without the awkwardness, saying those thoughts that couldn't be said at the time because the fog from the accident seemed to cloud the room.

The funerals of our parents had brought the family together. Even after the long struggle of Frank's mother to let go. But Daniel's death tore at us. We all went to the funeral held up in our little units of safety, or what we could manufacture of safety. There had been no feeling of unity at the funeral. We wanted to stand away from one another. There had even been release after the struggle of my father to hold on to his life. But there was only hard-nosed loss at Daniel's funeral.

"Some children you shouldn't let out of the crib," I remember saying.

A ziggurat is an escape hatch on a submarine.
A ziggurat is a rail for a troop train.
A ziggurat is a turf war.
A ziggurat is a pointy hat for whatever situation one finds oneself in.
A ziggurat is a video of the inner landscape.
A ziggurat is a cup for the guilty.
A ziggurat is the memory of a garden.

"I go to the work shed in the morning," I told them. Often, I don't know what I'm going to shape until I get there. The shaping of clay is the work of creation—only more so, because the creation has already been created. It then becomes a means of vision, a venue for vision, with differing venues. My anger at the hell Daniel put us through. Anger at my helplessness. Anger at God. Anger at Frank because he was powerless also. Anger that we had such frustration to endure. A ziggurat was the attempt of people to step off the earth. Before Daniel's accident, I made an inverted ziggurat. Something like a grave. I remember working at the table that morning in my shed. After his death, when I returned to work, I almost could see the dark road where Daniel's car slipped. Or maybe it was flung. I worked with the ziggurat I had started before Daniel's death. I didn't realize what it meant, but it became a part of the shadows around it. It was a viewing, as if through a telescope. Or maybe more like binoculars. To build something—to get to some understanding. In a ziggurat, I deal with the ineffectual, the condition in which I find myself.

I saw Thelma with her handkerchief to her nose as I talked.

After Daniel died, I felt like my ziggurat was a strip of land surrounded by water, though Fenton has no large body of water anywhere. I felt a parent's love that shook the ground like those enormous shovels that strip the earth of its coal.

The audience learned toward me as I talked. There was something about being in front of people in the pleasant room, surrounded by my ziggurats, a new scarf around my neck—the attention on me—their curiosity of how I made it through the horror, that opened me like the saw they used to cut Daniel out of the car.

No, no, you see, I'm coming to understand reversal. The body of water is my ziggurats, and I am the small strip of land between them.

I felt power to drive into myself. To talk about what I had not talked about. To take a saw that could cut through a car. A metal saw. I don't know what it looked like. I wasn't there. They had us wait at the morgue in the basement of the clinic in Fenton. I wanted to see Daniel, though Frank did not want me to. I wanted to see his battered face, the shards of glass still in his skin, his ear nearly torn from his face. The rest of him was covered by a sheet. I hold the body of ziggurats as if I could shape Daniel's body back into what it should have been. I would shape Daniel himself. The man. The coils of his thoughts. I would make them reasonable.

Daniel's Visions

I WAS RESTLESS AND could not sleep. Daniel's visions from the Bible came to me—his thoughts in his head on his bed. I saw a man made of metal. I saw trees with leaves that flew like bullets. Bats were helicopters with wings turning above their heads. I saw a black hole—not sucking Daniel into it as yet, but growing larger a layer at a time until it could swallow him and our whole world. It was a black hole with bat teeth.

My potter's wheel turned faster and faster and threw clay against the wall. Thwack. Thwack. When clay was fired, the holes grew smaller. But these holes became larger. Shapes and forms moved before my eyes as I tried to sleep. Was it Daniel Winscott trying to dance back into my thoughts? Was Daniel sharing his visions with me? Was he suggesting new forms I could use for my ziggurats?

I think we live with animals we can't see. Later that night I tried to sleep, thinking of animals that were brown: box turtle, wolf, fox, wren, dogsled. I was losing my track. Igloo (by now I was into white), snow goggle, seal skin. Eskimo, frigid. I woke and the air was all elephant tusk.

Other times, I get a glimmer of something small, round, and furry—possibly a muskrat. I want to live with wounded animals. The ones hurt by overbuilding with nowhere to go. Those who were trapped or exterminated.

No, I wanted my freedom from the needy ones. That sharp reversal came to my thoughts as I sat up in bed and walked down the dark hall to the window where I could see across the field into the distance.

I wanted to find the place where Daniel died. Frank had not been forthcoming about it. I'm sure the police told him the exact place. But Frank could not go to it yet, though it had been years. At times, I had a sense of mistrust toward Frank.

I wanted to make another trip to Daniel's grave, though driving was not my forte. I wanted to go by myself and stand there, telling him to depart from us. It was over. He'd had his time on earth, and now it was gone. He had given it away. Now he had to move on. He had to stop haunting us and haunting us. I've packed your bags. I gave away everything of yours still left in the house except the marbles, which I use in my work. I was cruel to him. I was tired of him. His excuses. His demands. His excesses. He had sucked the life out of us. You take and take from us and never give anything back except embarrassment and despair. No, Daniel was not here to help me create new forms for my work. He was here to terrorize me. To place guilt on my worktable until it was all I could see. What gives you the right? Get away. Move on. I felt a sharp wave of anger fuse over me. I handed my guilt back to him.

A Collapse

THEN IT HAPPENED. I had a small collapse. I could hardly walk. I could hardly talk. I was clay without anyone to form me. How did the body invent collapse? Did it just decide it was time to shut down for a while? I roused from my stupor. I was in a strange bed. Frank stood at the foot. I wanted to tell him I didn't want to do what they wanted me to. They didn't understand I was frantic. They roped me to the chair when they wanted me to sit there. They roped me to the bed when they wanted me to sleep. But sleep didn't come. Just a groggy after-light of consciousness. It was the drugs they gave me to calm the distress I felt. Let them be themselves on the inside, yet on the outside, be nothing but a lump of clay.

I wish I been more compliant. But that's what I did. I fought back. I scratched them. Pinched their arms when they got close enough. Then they put mittens on my hands so I couldn't use my fingers. Had madness finally overtaken me? I was rendered helpless with drugs and ropes. I struggled to get away. There was a large looming dark presence in the corner of the room with antennae on its head, just waiting for them to turn their back. Then it came at me with a vengeance. I cried for it to get back. They would come into the room and tie me once again. They put a beeper on my nightgown so that every time I moved it alerted them. If I moved too violently, they would be there. There were times I nearly made it free. Once I stood up beside the bed, but saw the wall tilting toward me. I hit my head on the heater and left a gash in my temple. I was sedated for the stitches. They shaved a side of my head for that.

Winnie came. I thought it was her. "Mother, Mother." She leaned over my bed. She looked at me like I was a stranger.

"I'm here," I said, but she looked at me as though I had said nothing. She was one of them too. I saw it now. Warren came. I told him also, but he didn't respond. I thought he would rip me from the room. Throw all of them back. Stomp the beetles that roamed the floor. I could smell them. I could hear them talk. I had so many children with me, and I could not feed them. What could I do? I cried and they ignored me. I asked for food for the children, and they did not understand. Did they think I could make all that up? I could not. How could they not know what was happening?

Winnie and Warren stood in the doorway talking to someone. Was it an old friend who had come to rescue? Was it Edwin Harsler who drove by? A pie in his car from a widow? I called to him for a ride. I think it was him, but he wouldn't stop. Why would Edwin be here? Was it Frank? Where was he? In his study translating a book already translated? What did he know? We are married to someone all our lives, and they are such little help. They are not there when we need them, and I am left to face the dark, throbbing being in the corner of the room that always pulls back when someone enters. I feel myself in its mouth, and then someone is here. Once, I thought they put a rag in my mouth so I could not shout.

"Don't shout," they said.

I would have a mouth to bite them if I were quiet. Or I could wait until I saw the dark one over me and scream at the last minute. I think sometimes they delayed their arrival. They knew the dark one was here. They wanted it to eat me. Maybe they had sent it to get rid of me because I was trouble.

They betray you. They have an idea of the way things are, but they are not. There's another way of seeing. It is frightful. All is at stake. Nothing is certain. Time is not in order.

Thelma stood there with her daughter, Lizbet. "John is here too," she said. But all I saw was a woman in the rain.

There were islands in the collapse. The temporary upset. "Dementia" is the word I heard them say. One island here. One island there. I could step between them and, on certain days, not drown.

Was I seeing what Daniel saw? Was my son the presence in the corner with the antennae on his head?

There were pockets of memory. My grandmother kneading dough as I stood beside her, eye-level to the table, watching the mound that yeast had built being pounded down to rise again. Maybe those mounds were the beginning of my ziggurats. Or my desire for ziggurats. Maybe that small memory rose with yeast, longing to rise in every ziggurat I made.

Where did I first see a ziggurat? How did I know about ziggurats? Frank, of course. I was a minister's wife. My children were ziggurats as they grew.

Much later, in New York City, when Frank and I were there, the children left with babysitters—with Uncle John and Aunt Thelma overseeing—and Edwin Harsler's wife having them all over to supper, and to play with Helen—Frank and I went to New York City for a national conference of his denomination.

The buildings were towers more than ziggurats, but it was ziggurats I saw from the plane. Once in the city, I stood dumbfounded at the structure of the Guggenheim.

When they stopped drugging me, I recovered my senses.

"Your system had an aversion to the medication. They had a misunderstanding."

"My blue woman was white," I told Frank. "There was a woman with me who was white.

"The nurses," Frank suggested. "They have white uniforms."

"No, I recognized the nurses," I told him. "She wasn't one of them."

"Maybe she was an aftermath of your breakdown."

"Don't call it that. I don't like the word."

"At least it wasn't a stroke," Frank said. "Maybe it was Lot's wife. You work too hard. It's a warning you should not look back."

"Lose a son on drugs and tell me how to do that."

"I lost him too."

Lot's Wife

And delivered just Lot, vexed with the filthy manner of life of the wicked.
—2 Pet 2:7-8

I WAS ON A new series of ziggurats. I wanted to work with interrelated forms. I looked through the religious art books in Frank's study. I researched Lot's daughters. There were several paintings of them, mostly having to do with the seduction of their father in a cave after the destruction of Sodom— Albrecht Durer's *Lot Fleeing with His Daughters from Sodom* and *Lot's Daughters in a Cave* by the Italian painter Carlo Carra.

"And there came two angels to Sodom at evening; and Lot sat in the gate of Sodom: and seeing them he rose to meet them; and he bowed himself with his face toward the ground" (Gen 19:1). He took them home, and the men of the city surrounded the house asking for them. Lot refused but offered them his two daughters instead. He knew the men wouldn't want them. That's why he offered. Imagine their horror underneath the justification.

In my inverted ziggurat series, I made a house for the two daughters of Lot.

With their eyes of fire, their hair of hacksaws, locusts entered their ears. In their mouths, a wasp's nest I found in a corner of the work shed.

Two daughters who have known no men. *Let me bring them out to you.*

The thought of us pushing Winnie out the door was abhorrent. What was the matter with Lot and his wife?

I made an inverted ziggurat for the two daughters of Lot. I could hear their voices calling from the clay as I worked. *Did he think we would go willingly? Did he think we would follow him from the house? We were his children, but he gave us away to be ravished.*

I heard their words over and over in my thoughts. It was the words I put in my ziggurat as I worked that morning.

The two men, or men who were angels, pulled Lot inside the door and closed it against the men in the street, which saved the daughters from being pushed into the crowd of men. And Irit, their mother? Would she have stood idly by at the screams of her daughters?

What would those men have done, if they had wanted women?

Do to them what is good in your eyes.

Ravishment is good? What was Lot saying?

I felt my legs tremble. My sister stood firmer. She knew they would not want women. But they might harm us anyway because we were not what they wanted. We were refuse. We heard our father's words, "Do nothing to the men, for they are under the shadow of my roof." Were we not protected there too? Was our father's roof a mere shadow? I continued to hear the daughters' reasoning.

The angels who looked like ordinary men took Lot by the arm and drew him into the house and shut the door. They smote the men at the door with blindness, or a blind confusion so that they couldn't find the door.

And our mother? She could have spoken. But what would she have said? To speak up would have brought reproach. Or could she have spoken in spite of the reproach, but chose not to? Would she have been in trouble if she did, and in trouble if she hadn't?

And Lot went out and spoke to his sons-in-law who married his daughters and said, *Get out of this place—the Lord will destroy the city*. But they didn't believe him.

Were the daughters his only two daughters? Or did he have other daughters who were the wives of his sons-in-law? How could he offer his two daughters who have not known men (Gen 19:8)?

There's an inconsistency, I would tell Frank and Uncle John Winscott. Let them answer that one. But I didn't want to bother them. I heard them at work trying to fasten a gutter to the house that had come loose. I saw Edwin Harsler's car through the window of my work shed. It would take all three of them to attach the gutter. It would take more than the three of them to keep the house from falling down. What was a house but a series of repairs until repairs could not be made anymore? We couldn't afford new gutters and had listened to the splat of rain off the house in a storm until the runoff made a burrow in the ground.

Lot's Wife

Maybe Lot's two daughters were married, but had not slept with their husbands. Therefore they were wives but had known no man. Or were their husbands something they did not know because they had not been taken into their confidence? Or did Lot have four daughters, two of whom were married and two unmarried?

"I think the daughters had not been taken into their husbands' confidence," I said at lunch, "the way, Frank, when you are lost in your translations, I am invisible to you. I do not know you. I don't know what moves your blasted interest in translating an untranslatable work."

"But it is translatable," Frank said, ignoring my direct address to him in front of John and Edwin. "Translation is a table that moves with many turns."

"How many, Frank?"

"As many turns as those turning it," he said

"Blast it, Frank. Don't you know I would be like Lot's wife and look at the burning city? I would rather be a pillar of salt. I am that to you at times."

"No, Euge, you're not. If you were, I could post you in the backyard— bring you in from time to time in a hard rain. It would be easier then answering your continual questions."

"You are on your continent. I am on my island. These words are a current between them." I saw Uncle John Winscott shift uncomfortably in his chair. Edwin Harsler, on the other hand, leaned forward to hear more.

There was an old prophet whom God told not to return to where he'd been, but another prophet came and said it was all right. The old prophet returned and was killed by a lion (1 Kgs 13:1–24). I knew, therefore, not to return to my attack, though I told myself I could. Edwin Harsler was waiting for it.

"'If anyone, man or angel, preaches anything different than I have learned, let him be accursed' (Gal 1:9)."

"Well, those are words of fire that could be spoken by any infidel," I said, though I knew my argument was not making sense.

"An infidel in your religion. But not mine."

Rock City

THERE IS A ROCK city that lies with us. I woke one morning with that revelation. What did it mean?

I stood on my thoughts, those little sticks that could bend in a moment—that could twist and break. How many had I used in my ziggurats for antennas or tubing? No, I decided, my convictions were solid. The conscience was a rock city. Wasn't it one of Warren's girlfriends who had said that of my ziggurats? What was her name? How many of his girlfriends—and how many of his plans had blown away as twigs in the wind? I felt the foundation of that rock city within. I had worked to bring outward in the world what I had found within.

"We have a conscience without God," I tried to argue once. But Frank gave me an answer about the instability or the mutability of the conscience without God. That was his opinion.

To bisque is to fire the clay for the first time. Afterward, the glazes. The craze of cracks. The different stains that run through them. Another thousand degrees of fire to turn the clay into a city of rocks.

Flaw

MAYBE DANIEL HAD BEEN born with a propensity for addiction. Maybe some are born with flaws that will bring us closer to the edge. My Grandfather Nyland had a horse with a crooked tooth that became abscessed with age and turned to cancer. A muscle weakness came upon my father later in life. He remembered it had been with him as a child. But my flaw was more sinister. A flaw in the character. Maybe I had inherited it from them. My father lived without any thought of God. It seemed normal. It was Frank's dip into the ocean of Scripture that seem out of place.

Was I having flashbacks to my temporary dementia? Do you know what it's like to know you are there? To know you have stepped into a different realm? A realm within yourself where you shouldn't be. Once you've been there, you're not entirely free of it.

"It still seems everything we need to know," I picked up on Frank's conversation. I assume he was talking about the Bible with Uncle John.

An embedded tooth. A swelling of the jaw. A denial of Christ.

"The words of faith I could have spoken. The choice I made not to speak. Not to hear. To ignore. But it was still there."

"So it is according to our belief? If I believe it is there, it is. If I don't believe, then it isn't," Frank was saying.

"I wouldn't be sure of that," Uncle John Winscott said.

"Has anyone returned from the dead?"

"Christ. Lazarus. Dorcas. A small girl—who was she? Jarias' daughter? There were others."

"Daniel will not be one of them who returns from the dead," Frank bemoaned.

"I would have to answer for my life. There is a judgment seat," John Winscott said.

"Where does it say that?" I asked.

"In the Bible."

"Well, eliminate the Bible, and you eliminate hell," I conceded.

"Can you eliminate death?" Frank asked. "It says in the Bible there is once to live and once to die."

"You aren't afraid?"

"Not unreasonably so."

Journal entry, June 25: *A rock is a boulder in hell.*

Daniel's Funeral

Frank had preached Daniel's funeral with dignity. I was grateful to everyone who stood in the rain. Uncle John Winscott had wanted to take the funeral, but Frank wouldn't listen. I was on Uncle John's side, but Frank was determined. I don't know how he did it. I was choked with tears. My throat felt like it had a fireball in it. I coughed once, but it seemed to lodge deeper.

I was aware of the crowd of people around us. Frank's congregation and townspeople from Fenton. I saw the Figgetts and their friends. There were others I didn't know. Some of them probably relatives. Uncle John and Thelma stood beside us. John II, Thomas, and Lizbet, along with their children, stood behind Warren and Winnie. The Woodruffs were there, who had put our house and yard in order. Edwin Harsler and Helen, his daughter. I looked past them at a woman who lowered her umbrella to cover her face when I looked at her. And there was a man. I had seen him before, fading into the background when I looked. Who was he? The man who seemed to belong, yet was not a part of any group. He was sinister. A friend of Daniel's? Something was wrong with him. Something was wrong with him being there. He looked away when I stared at him.

I turned my attention back to the funeral, with the rain trying to wash us all clean.

Somehow, the funeral was over. We stumbled to the church. There was food, though Frank and I could not eat. We visited with the funeral guests, not knowing what we said. Finally, we stumbled back to our house and took off our damp shoes and clothes.

Frank wasn't the same after Daniel's funeral. He didn't defend the faith to me as much as he had. Somehow I saw the hand of God in Daniel's death. He was now cared for in heaven. I could convince myself of that, but Frank could not.

"I'm not sure anymore that's where he is," he said, choked with grief.

After Daniel's funeral, Frank couldn't read after the sun went down, though he sat under his study lamp with its two hundred-watt light bulb. He said the words blurred on the page. He couldn't concentrate. We sat together after dark. We listened to the radio. We dozed in our chairs until I dragged Frank to bed, where I felt him toss through the night. He was wrestling with his faith. He was winning. Yet he couldn't find his old zeal when we argued over the Bible.

He was a stranger to the words he delivered at the funeral. I think he resented a God who had not intervened in Daniel's addiction. I think he preached truth, while he felt untruth. It caused a small cut in his faith that seemed to grow infected.

A loving God had removed our wayward son. A loving, judgmental God with power to remove. That was the hard root on which we had to chew while *it was an accident* buzzed in our heads. Judgment. Accident. Judgment. Accident. No—it was the natural outcome of the choices Daniel made, Frank mulled. An outcome of his addiction. We still went back and forth. Accident. Judgment. Judgment. Accident. It all mashed together in our heads.

Back Flash

"Isn't it time for lunch?"

"Frank, make your own sandwich," I answered. "I can't be making your lunch every day."

"You fuss about the mess I make."

"Open a can of soup. Warm it on the stove. Pour a bowl for me also."

He turned away from the door of the work shed. I felt a path of guilt right up the center of my being. What was I supposed to do? Stop my creative efforts and fix soup for a man who was capable of opening the fridge and finding the lunchmeat and cheese and putting them on bread? What was the matter with him? Why did he ask? Maybe he needed company. Maybe I needed more time away from the work shed, but I decided to let him fend for himself. In the jungle of the kitchen, I would let him battle for his lunch.

> Journal entry, August 1: *I thought of writing words to Daniel on my ziggurat. What did I do to you? I couldn't carry you beyond childhood. Why didn't you go on your own? Where is it you've gone? Is there no way back? Who are you talking to those nights I hear you mutter?*

"Have you thought about what we're going to do for dinner?" Frank asked when I returned to the house in the afternoon.

"Yes, Frank. I usually plan the week's meals in my head. I've been doing it for years. I don't need to plan it outright. It just comes. When I'm at the store, I have categories of variety. This one week. Not again for two. Or this salad with this main course. Or that with this. Zucchini bread one week. Pumpkin bread the next. I know you're ingrained that way. It follows like chapters in your book. Someday I'll stand at your grave and apologize for all the meals I fed you late. I'll apologize for all my carelessness and shortcomings. I will inhabit the rings of hell."

"Do you think you move around in hell, visiting one rung or another? The way we ascended and descended the Guggenheim? Have you considered that you may be chained to one spot for eternity?"

"You're asking some pointed questions," I said. "If we're lost and don't know where we are, that's part of the hell of it."

"I thought you might know, spending so much time in your ziggurats as you do."

"I imagine we could travel, but we don't want to," I answered. "I imagine it would be too arduous, too tremendous an effort. It would leave us panting for another ten thousand years." I looked at Uncle John Winscott, whom I hadn't realized was there, and continued, "Then there's the problem that we might get lost."

"Lost on a ziggurat?"

"Well, there are little chambers within the slanted walkway. To get lost would be another hell indeed. A hell within a hell."

"There, you've said it." John Winscott was excited. "It's all imaginary. Shifting. You've already changed positions, which weakens your case."

"It's not my case, but God's," Frank said.

"It seems like you're doing a lot of interpreting for God," I remarked. "Are you like one of those old prophets who spoke directly with God and said, 'thus says the Lord'?"

"My prophecy is from the Bible," Frank answered. "I simply repeat what it says."

"The mouth of the Bible."

"A hint at what is there," Frank said. "I don't understand all its meanings. But the core ones I get: we are at a loss without Christ."

"But you more than hint. You seem blastedly certain of it all. Your heaven and hell."

"It's not mine. I only hope to be there someday," Frank said. "I want to be in the crowd of worshippers."

"And what do you do up there?"

"I suppose I will worship Christ. I will travel through space. I will see the wonders that are so wonderful we can't know them here, or else we would not be able to abide our place here."

"You've got it wrapped up," I said.

"Yes, the wrapping is called the Bible."

"Well, stand there in your black leather cover and ride away."

"I will be sorry to leave you behind."

Thelma was coming for supper that evening. She didn't bother me when she knew I was working on a project, which was most of the day. I felt bad sometimes because I was not more of a companion for her, or for anyone, for that matter.

There seemed to be a louder noise than Thelma's usual demure arrival. From the window, I saw that Edwin Harsler had followed Thelma up the drive.

"Thought I'd see how you were doing." Edwin kissed me on the side of my head as I came to the house from the work shed.

"Won't you stay for supper?" I asked.

Thelma put on an apron, and we began to prepare the meal.

At dinner we discussed a child murdered by his mother's boyfriend. On a television program, Thelma had seen a polar bear eating one of his cubs. I mentioned a deer driving others away from the corn that Frank threw on the edge of the yard at the end of winter when they had little to eat. The birds scrapping at the feeders.

Frank left verses on my work table. They were verses he used to provoke me. I felt I made more stirring ziggurats when I was stirred.

"Take heed to yourself that you make no carved images . . . the similitude of any figure . . . the likeness of any beast on earth . . . the likeness of any winged fowl that flies in the air . . . the likeness of anything that creeps on the ground . . . the likeness of any fish that is in the waters beneath the earth . . . the likeness of the sun, moon, stars in the heavens" (Deut 4:15–20 KJV and NRSV).

Yes, Frank poked my guilt. I was making images, indeed. I carved him into one of the rims of the ziggurat. I cut strips from one of his neckties for the ziggurat.

I was making similitudes. I was making fury.

Maybe I could write Biblical passages on them, like William Blake's illustrations of the book of Job.

I was sorry to be curt. I didn't want to use the Bible as a roller blade. I wanted to use it to scrape the frost away from his eyes.

It is hard to understand. To believe. I make it a point not to, though I spent more time in the Bible refuting Frank than he spent defending it and making his blasted interpretations.

The word of God abides in him. Who does not believe? Me. I fear my restlessness will torment me. It is all I have without any respite. Frank says that's what hell is. Eternal restless, pain and torture, thirst and hunger. The unrelenting grief of being left out, of knowing another decision could be made. But here I have the loneliness of insubstantial thought. I fear only my empty mind and the memory of a child who died. Hell is a son on drugs. Hell is knowing there is a God who could have spared that son, but God was not in the sparing business. Look what he let happen to his own Son.

Deaf and blind—locked in the meandering stream of one's own head, as E.L. Doctorow explained in the back of his book, *Homer and Langley*, a book I had borrowed from the Fenton library. It was the unremitting consciousness that knows only itself. I was sorry to be curt.

I didn't want to return to passages in the Bible because they bit.

Daniel took drugs to awaken a spiritual understanding. What really happened? He found he was an addict. He was nothing but helpless before God. To be taken by self is a kind of hell. To be taken by the will is self. Hell is self-absorption.

"In the church I went to as a girl, they didn't ask about salvation," Thelma said.

"For me, the abundant life is to work with ziggurats," I said and waited for Frank's glare.

"I finally heard the message and accepted it," Thelma said. "Christ took my sins upon himself and died with them on the cross so he would have a redeemed people."

I listened as they went over the Bible that translated itself out of meaning for me.

I took some of the names for my ziggurats from Frank's work.

Back Flash

Merononthite. Horonite. Sanballat. Meremoth. Those names were from the book of Nehemiah where the people worked rebuilding the walls of Jerusalem, their swords by their sides as they worked (Neh 4:18).

At times, I stopped to write in my journals, *Ziggurats and Me*. I kept them on the sagging bookshelves in my work shed, like a weapon at my side. I took notes on my process of forming ziggurats. I wrote about vision. I kept a list of new ideas for the shapes of ziggurats. I noted possibilities, hauntings, relativities. I kept other notes: "Some woke to the resurrections of damnation" (John 5:29).

Sometimes the mail truck brought letters and postcards from the children, but mostly Winnie and Warren took the shortcut and e-mailed us. I always could hear the squeak of brakes at our mailbox. Sometimes the mail truck brought us Edwin Harsler. He seemed to follow it around the country. It was the only time I looked up from the salt pillars of my ziggurats.

I dreamed that someone was raking leaves. Under the leaves was Daniel's grave. Daniel, our son, killed by a mistake in driving. One moment of inattention and he was gone. It didn't seem fair. What world was I living in? What world was he? His head fogged with drugs, he was using them as insecticide to rid himself of all those bugs flying into his head, caused by drugs in the first place. His inoculations were actually the cause of the disease.

I woke shivering with a dream my children were turning into ziggurats. I woke thinking of Daniel—his head flogged with drugs.

There was time when I wasn't married. My name was Eugena Nyland. There was a time when I didn't wrap myself in ziggurats. Why was I drawn to them in the first place? They were escape.

Was this a dream? Was I dreaming on the other side? Making a patchwork of images the way my grandmother used scraps of our old clothes for her quilts?

I layered myself. I had my work. My past. My outings to Fenton. My kitchen. My own place in my work shed where I could be by myself because Frank was by himself in the study. At one time we had traveled many places together. Sometimes I got out the albums and my notes on ziggurats that I had taken while traveling.

"Teraphim," Frank said, "small household gods—that's what your ziggurats were."

I thought of making them large. I thought of a ziggurat that filled my work shed.

> Journal entry, August 6: *The trees slept standing up like horses. Other times, I found them on their sides.*

What could I make of that, so many years later?

"It's the medication that makes you see what isn't here," they had said. But what I saw was there. Maybe Daniel was trying to keep from running over something he saw that night, and he swerved and went off the road.

"*If you don't take me to that place!*" I said to Frank.

Of Frank: his neglect of me over the Bible. Living in his head as he does. Couldn't he come down into the other parts of his body? His heart, for instance?

I should list my own shortcomings when I think of his. I stay in my work shed when I know it is late and he is hungry. I shape the clay the way I want without considering "the Potter," as Frank calls him.

"Pray for others, even our enemies," Frank insisted. He prayed for a boy who bullied our son, Warren. He prayed for a girl who jilted Daniel.

"Did you pray for the devil that deceived him?" I asked bitterly. "Did you pray for the dealers and suppliers?" They torture us with letters and notes accusing Daniel of debt we should pay. We have paid, I would say to them. We have paid. They can take their drugs and back off. Blow. Freeze. Monster. Crack. Hardball. Casper. Base. Beat. Scrabble. Stone. Tornado. Stoppers. Red bullets. Apache. China girl. Dance fever. Tango. Cherry soap. Good fellows. Aunt Hazel. Big H. Black pearls. Mud. Tar. Horse. Smack. Bolt. Boppers. Moon gas. Pink robots. Cubes. Skunk. Blue kiss. How many names fed my ziggurats?

Back Flash

I wanted to talk to Frank, but he was at work to clarify, to handle, to control. What did Frank get wrong? What made him do what he did? Did he have an overbearing father who demanded perfection? Did he get an answer wrong at one time and was severely punished? Or shamed in front of others so that he vowed he would never be wrong again? What was behind his hours of research? Of moving words around to see what else they could say? What did he have to prove?

All of this is not what sent me here—into the hell of my thoughts—but refusal of Jesus Christ. I don't like anyone who has to have their own way.

A Brief Confrontation

I was on my way to Fenton when I noticed the car in front of me. It was behind another car that slowed as it neared town. There was a man in the car. He seemed familiar. Where had I seen him? Was he the man I saw at Daniel's funeral?

I followed the car for several blocks past the stores, the library, the hardware store, the bed-and-breakfast, the Art and Cultural Center. When he got out at the post office, I stopped behind him.

"Were you a friend of Daniel's?" I confronted him on the walk.

"I don't know anyone named Daniel."

"Daniel Winscott. Yes, you do."

He didn't answer.

"Were you with Daniel before he died? Do you know why he was on the road that night by himself? Where was he going?"

The man tried to walk past me.

"I know you know something," I huffed.

He went into the post office, and I followed.

"I saw you on the square that day when I was with my husband. I didn't stop because I didn't want to upset Frank. I'm Daniel's mother, you know. Are you a dealer? Did you supply Daniel with drugs?"

"No, madam, I did not."

"I saw you at Daniel's funeral."

"I doubt that a dealer goes to the funerals of his clients."

"Who are you then?"

He tried to ignore me.

"A lover?"

"No."

"A conspirator?"

He tried to look past me.

A Brief Confrontation

"Tell your friends *to stop sending us letters.*"

People in line in the post office were staring at us. The man would not talk to me. In his exasperation, he left. I followed him to his car. I looked at his front fender to see if it was dented—to see if it had pushed anyone off the road. I tried to open the car door when he closed it, but he drove off.

A friend who'd been at Fenton's Art and Cultural Center that day walked me to the curb.

"Why are you after him?"

"He's a man who handles bats," I explained.

Ironic Witness

"The grid of the Bible—it's all mathematical." Frank's Uncle John had his theories. I listened to them in the kitchen as I cleared the breakfast dishes.

"But not like *The Divine Comedy*," Frank interjected, "three canticles of thirty-three cantos of three-line tercets. Three-by-three all the way."

I hated them for the freedom they had from ziggurats. Yet I only wanted to think about ziggurats. I did not want to be free from them. There was something fundamental about them. A mystery I wanted to stay with. I wanted to name the ziggurats like Adam named the animals. I wanted to think about the mathematics of ziggurats.

In my work shed that morning, a family vacation to the Atlantic came to mind. Not the Gulf, where we usually went, but a long trip to the east coast. I remembered Daniel, Winnie, and Warren, probably aged twelve, nine, and seven, running on the shore with their little buckets filled with shells that stank on the screened porch of the house we rented. We had to wash them, then dry them in the sun several days, and still we smelled them from the trunk of the car on our way back. Frank stopped once to sort through the bags for the foulest smelling ones, and finding the culprits, tossed them to the side of the road while Winnie screamed in the back seat for her shells.

I could smell traces of the ocean in the children's rooms for a long time, especially Winnie's room; she had the biggest collection in a bowl by the window. One morning I looked through them to find the hermit crab shell with small geometric stripes—red nerite was its name—a shell raised like a ziggurat. Even the sea worked to shape their mystery.

I made small ziggurats like those shells. I made larger ziggurats like ocean waves spilling into shore. They looked like ziggurats someone had pushed to the side. Or tried to sit on. They listed like the Tower of Pisa, only worse.

Ironic Witness

"Do horses run on rocks? Do you plow there with oxen?

—Amos 6:11–12 KJV

"What is it today?" I asked while I was fixing lunch. Frank and Uncle John Winscott were in the book of Amos. I was chopping onions while they talked.

"What's the matter, Eugena? You're chopping with fury."

"I'm thinking of Daniel. I'm thinking of a road covered with rain, slick as a peeled onion. I'm thinking of an unfair God."

"Shall horses run upon the rocks?" I wrote on the side of my ziggurats that afternoon.

Here on the isthmus of myself in the work shed, I often regretted how much Frank's studies informed my work. I think how often I used his words in my ziggurats. Even if I used them for my refutations of his words.

I had clay up to my elbows, clay covering my work apron and my work shoes. The walls of the work shed seemed to become clay. The whole work shed itself seemed to transform itself into a living being made of clay.

As it turned out, I did not name every ziggurat. Some of the ziggurats had names no one knew, not even me. I would look at a ziggurat. I would look at it in relationship to the other ziggurats. I listened to what I was thinking. I listened to the baggage that came with it. What else it reminded me of. What words were coming? What responses? What else was going on? What snatches of Frank and Uncle John Winscott's conversations? What had happened in the news? What was the essence that stood apart from the ziggurat? Sometimes, ironically, they reminded me of heaven, though I had no clear idea of what that was, except a ziggurat going on forever.

In winter, I saw the hoarfrost on the edge of the window. I felt its coarseness. It almost was prickly. Adam must have touched the hard neck of the large brown animal and said, "horse." Of course, he did not speak English. It would have been a sound from his own language. And what was his language? Hebrew? Or some form of it? Did he have to take language lessons, or were some sounds from a speech impediment as he was learning language, maybe God adjusting his jaw, a little here and a little there? Was he born knowing language? No, Adam wasn't born. He was formed of the clay of the ground and the breath of God. He was God's ziggurat.

The Blue Scarf

WHEN I WAS A girl, my parents argued. Often, we returned from my grandparents' farm in a ball of frustration. What was it about those trips that upset my parents?

My mother was a handsome woman. Maybe my father was jealous. I inherited his plainness. Once, I tied my mother's blue silk scarf around my neck. I meant to return it, but it was like touching water. It was like pulling the ocean through my hands. I remember the repetition of its waves.

How often my parents tried to plow the rocks.

Once in the barn, a bat stuck to my hair. Or is it in hell?

Would my father have been an addict if Daniel's drugs were available to him?

Frank agreed to let Edwin Harsler drive us in our car to the place where Daniel died. As we drove through Fenton and turned north, I was thinking of the absolute darkness in the farmhouse when we visited my grandparents. I tried to think of Daniel on the road in such darkness. The police had given Frank the location. I knew they did. Frank didn't know if he could take me by himself. What if I got hysterical? What if he did? I asked.

It was a state road north of Fenton. I remembered it from before it was paved. We'd driven that way on various journeys, though not often. In the old days, we used to go on rides—Sunday afternoon rides, sometimes Saturday afternoon rides to have something to do with the children. For some reason they liked to ride in the car.

The curving road made me dizzy. I asked Edwin to slow the car. I knew why he could cover the country the way he did. Several miles ahead, he slowed, looking into the brush beside the road. Frank told him it was farther. Past the leaning mailbox and the farmhouse hidden in the trees. Past the poplars hissing in the wind. I leaned forward in the backseat to see between Edwin and Frank. I thought again of the darkness of my grandparents' farmhouse. The absolute darkness when the sun went down before they had electricity. Maybe the moon, if it was full, provided a dimness. But I remembered the dark.

"Here," Edwin said.

Frank looked at the ravine at the side of the road. "I think it was deeper than this one because the car wasn't visible from the road."

"It was the dense trees that hid it, not the ravine."

"Daniel was out of sight for several days," Frank said.

"Cars that pass on this curve are looking at the road. They don't have time to look into the ravine."

"It was headlights reflecting on the metal. Someone saw it. Someone stopped and called the police."

Edwin drove to the next bend in the road where another ravine dropped sharply into a slope that continued into the woods. I could understand how an accident could happen. Especially to someone whose faculties were clouded by drugs—someone with a person behind him in another car, trying to hurry him along. Or threatening him, even pushing him.

"You can't stop on a curve. Turn around and come back," Frank instructed Edwin.

So Daniel was returning to Fenton. I thought he was leaving. He'd been somewhere and was trying to get back.

Edwin found a place to park. We'd have to walk back, but at least the car was visible if someone came suddenly around the bend.

It was hard to walk on the side of the road. Several cars passed. Soon, Frank indicated a tree with a gash in it, about the height of a car's bumper. There were broken branches. One bush was sheared off at the ground. Most of the underbrush had grown back.

"This is where it happened. This is where he died." Frank was matter-of-fact.

"Maybe he was dead on impact," I said, looking for calmness in my voice also. "I couldn't think of him stranded out here."

"No, the coroner said he survived a few hours at least."

Edwin Harsler looked on the ground for clues. He always irritated me. The clues I wanted weren't there at the bottom of the ravine. They were back on the road where Daniel was behind the wheel. But there were no skid marks on the road. The gravel on the side of the road showed the first signs of someone trying to break. There were tire marks where Frank moved the grass with his foot. I stood in the shade of the trees as Edwin ferretted in the grass—finding broken glass, shards of metal. Daniel. Daniel. Here was your exit from the earth. What did I expect? *The Journal of Daniel Winscott* exploring his life, his failures and shortcomings, and explaining his death? Did I expect answers to what happened? What calls had been made on his cell before the accident, before his service was shut off for nonpayment? What clues as to where he had been and why?

When we climbed back up the ravine, there in the ground were the tracks of another car.

"I think someone pushed him off the road."

"No," Frank said to me. "Don't make that up—" Frank was going to say something else but stopped. I heard the crack in his voice that would come if he continued.

"It could be the tow truck that pulled the car back on the road. Or one of the emergency vehicles," Edwin said.

I would have disagreed, but I couldn't speak either. I felt something like a blue silk scarf tightening around my neck. The pieces of words I wanted to say choking in my windpipe.

Off the Road

AFTER DANIEL DIED, I was in my work shed one morning, staring at my worktable. Frank came in the door that was ajar, reminding me I should keep the door closed. Otherwise, the insects would stick to my wet clay.

"Here it is, Eugena," he seemed to ignore my catatonic state, or near catatonic. I only wanted to stare at the table and see nothing. "'By the word of God the heavens were of old, and the earth standing out of the water and in the water' (2 Pet 3:5 KJV)." I was aware of his words to me, trying to draw me back from the edge of despair. I think I nearly felt Daniel's hands on me, trying to drag me to the pit with him. He needed company. Daniel or Frank? I think it was both. But I heard Frank talking somewhere. "By which the world that then was, being overflowed with water, perished. But the heavens and the earth which are now, by the same word are kept in store, reserved until fire against the days of judgments in the kiln."

I looked at Frank. "A kiln is there?"

"No, Eugena. I added that to get your attention."

"Is it time for lunch?" I asked. "You know how to make a sandwich."

"It's time for you to come out of your stupor."

"I feel him with me sometimes."

"I do too," Frank agreed.

"He wants back. He wasn't ready to leave."

"Maybe none of us are."

"I feel him knocking on the door," I said.

"Is that why you leave the door of your work shed ajar, letting in all kinds of insects?"

"I want to take his hand away from my arm," I told Frank. "I feel like he'd pull me away with him."

"Yes, he probably would," Frank admitted, "but that's not his decision. The power of life and death is with God."

"Daniel had a hand in his own death."

"Imagine the earth standing out of the water and in the water. Imagine a primeval state of being—the beginning of our six thousand year history on earth."

"Frank, there's carbon dating. There's evidence of events farther back than six thousand years. You know it's 4.5 billion."

"Of course. I see the upheaval of bedrock. The fragments of bones and fossils. But our dispensation began when God re-spoke the world into being. At first there was a heaven and earth, then something happened, and the earth was without form and darkness was on the water. Then God re-spoke: 'Let there be light.' He spoke it into being all over again."

"What point are you going to make, Frank?" I asked. "Does the Bible say 're-spoke'?"

"Image the earth standing out of the water and in the water. Do you remember when we drove through Pennsylvania several years ago? Was it our return from the Atlantic? The morning sun through the fog? The fog between the valleys? The hills standing above the fog? The earth felt lifted above itself."

"Frank, that was twenty years ago," I said. "Probably more than that."

"It was?"

"The children couldn't sit in the backseat without fighting." I reminded him. "They were bored with such a long trip. It wasn't as much fun as an afternoon ride, but it had the purpose of getting somewhere. Winnie finally had to sit with me in the front seat, remember? Her brothers were banished to each side of the backseat," I stopped. "It had to have been longer than fifteen years ago. It probably was twenty. Maybe more."

"'I saw earth without form, and the heavens had no light. I saw the mountains tremble. I saw there was no man, and all the birds had fled. I saw a wilderness, and all its cities were broken down at the presence of the Lord, by his fierce anger' (Jer 4:23 KJV)."

"My God, Frank," I interrupted. "Don't we have enough disaster in our lives? You have to ship it in from the Bible too?"

I was impatient with him. Why didn't he leave me alone? When did he help, standing there in his Bible clothes? His clown costume. I could have pulled it off with my teeth. I saw he understood what I was thinking. He stood there before me a moment in his rumpled shirt and trousers, his hair not combed since he had gotten out of bed that morning.

"You'll live in hell if you don't repent," Frank warned.

I felt the waters leaking from that old world, seeping out through my eyes.

> Journal entry, September 12: *Frank, why don't you speak to me on your own? Why do you always speak to me in quotes from the Bible? Why is God always between us? Don't you know how I miss your face against mine? Your words only to me?*

"Think of the earth as one of those blue marbles with cloud swirls the boys used to play with," Frank said. "Think of it out there in the blackness— with only the hand of God for help. Think of the black energy expanding outward."

I dreamed there were two attics above the attic of the house I didn't know were there.

I dreamed there were two attics above the attic above the second story. It was a different shape, not rectangular, but was roaming into other shapes. Was the house becoming a ziggurat? Did its history take on a physical presence? More than once, I dreamed of the baggage it carried on its head.

"Sometimes I hear Daniel crying," Frank said. "'Let us reason together,' the Lord must have said to him at one time, but Daniel wouldn't listen."

"'Let us reason together' means 'Let me persuade you to do it my way,'" I said.

"Did Daniel understand what he was doing?" Frank argued. "Maybe his name was too much for him to attain."

"Yes, Frank, it's our fault because we named him Daniel," I admitted with an edge. "You sound like Winnie whining about her name."

"It's us too."

"What do you mean?" I asked.

"Daniel is a mirror," he said, and I left the room.

Uncle John Winscott's Funeral

IT WAS WINTER. THEN it was summer. Then winter again. They seemed to change places before I knew it. This dreary business of aging and death. It was a muddle. It was confusion. It was a matter of ineptitude. There were a number of closings, some more painful than others, such as the morning Thelma called in tears and said that John had died in his sleep. I thought at first she was dying because of the gulps she made as she talked. Finally, I understood it was John. I wondered if Daniel had gulped too, when he tried to call out to someone for help, if he was still conscious after his wreck.

A large group of people gathered at the cemetery in the Winscott family plot. Some of the distant relatives I had not seen in a while. Thelma's children, John II, Thomas, and Lizbet, plus their spouses and children stood with Thelma at John's grave. The latest granddaughter, whatever her name, wore a cap that Thelma had knit. Our own children, Winnie and Warren, stood on either side of me as though I needed to be propped up. Some young man stood on the other side of Winnie. He had visited before. He had been the recent subject of her e-mails.

I was aware of Daniel as I listened to Frank's words. Daniel's grave was just behind me and to the south. I had picked up a pinecone and placed it by his headstone before Winnie took my arm and pulled me toward John's newly dug grave. Without my glasses, the pinecone looked like a small ziggurat.

After Frank's sermon, we had supper in the church we attended. Frank was tired. Warren and Thomas stood at his sides, holding his arm. Finally they got him seated. The voices of the scuffling children bothered me. I looked at the door, longing to leave.

"A life in the church must be rewarding," someone said to me.

"I had no choice," I said. "Neither did the children."

"Daniel is saved," I said to Frank later, after Winnie and Warren had left. "He accepted Christ. You said you heard him."

"No, he didn't," Frank said. "It was just words. He didn't know what he was saying. He only repeated what I wanted him to."

"But that counts. He was in church all those years."

"He didn't have a choice. As a minister's wife, you didn't have a choice."

"I wanted to be in church," I said. "There was something about sitting there with the children with you before us in the pulpit, with Daniel, Winifred, and Warren, lined up beside me."

"We should be convicted of our sin. So we can change."

"Do you think God took Daniel out because of his disobedience?"

"I don't know," Frank said.

"In the beginning, when he got high, he said he felt what he'd wanted to feel in church."

"He deceived himself," Frank stated.

"There are accidents," I said. "Sometimes there are just accidents."

"What keeps you in church?" Frank asked.

"I can go to church and think of ziggurats," I said. "I think it's where I first heard of them."

"What do you remember about my sermons, Eugena?" Frank asked.

"Are you going over your life thinking what a failure you've been?" I asked. "I'm sure you are," I continued, "Don't forget how you held a church together. Don't forget the students at the university you gave your wisdom to. Don't forget the good you've done." I liked being in church. I could go inside myself and be with myself there.

I had terrible dreams for nights after Uncle John Winscott's funeral. I saw upheaval. There was shooting in the streets. Anyone in the way was murdered. Then they went into houses to kill the people hiding there. Who were they? Soldiers of some kind. What was loose in the streets? What had happened to the world? No, what had happened to America? What had caused the drastic change?

Uncle John Winscott's Funeral

For several days after the nightmares, I worked on a ziggurat called *The Dark One*. In my dreams, I felt its hand petting my hair—raking my head with its fingers, making me quiver with disgust. There were visages of something else. A wall? It was as if someone licked different postage stamps and stuck them to the wall in a collage or pastiche of postage stamps for wallpaper.

These ziggurats are little evidences. Or insights. No, more like snapshots of my nightmares. There is a time coming. There is a time yet ahead.

There were days I worked because I felt something like panic. I had to work quickly, harder and harder, lest it overtake me. I was running out of time. I was running.

Woe to the coming time. When my ziggurats sounded like Old Testament prophets, I pulled out their tongues. I flattened them against my worktable. I put them in the oven.

I saw a change in Frank after Daniel's death. But it was after Uncle John Winscott's death that Frank went farther away each day into senility. He drooled. Crumbs covered his face and shirt. When he didn't shave, they stuck in his stubble. His wild hair stood on end. He didn't want it combed. He stared into the distance in his study. The doctor prescribed medication again for depression. He was admitted into assisted living in the senior center. I couldn't care for him. I drove to see him daily. Or Edwin took me. Thelma also was available, suggesting that I join him.

One evening Thelma pushed too far.

"I'm not going. I won't leave this place. What would I do all day? It would take my breath from me."

She was right. I couldn't keep up with the house. Mrs. Woodruff was no longer able to vacuum. The house had been in need of repair for years. The roof leaked. The yard was full of weeds. An upstairs toilet had been shut off. I had to walk downstairs in the night. I couldn't afford repairs. The dryer didn't work. I would hang up the few clothes I washed. Hadn't I used the clothesline in the old days? Frank even bought a night jar at Fenton's hardware. I wouldn't use it, but chose to descend the stairs.

"What about sheets?" Thelma asked.

I could tell Warren and Winnie were alarmed when they visited. Maybe they were working with Thelma to get me out of the house.

"I'll put them in a bundle and you can wash them for me if you want them clean."

We looked at one another. "I could be removed forcefully," she said. "Look at the clutter. Look at the dirt." When had I last swept? When had I dusted?

By that time, Warren and Winnie came with their spouses. What should they do with their parents? I saw it on their faces. I was a problem rather than solution. When had I made that change? What could I do? God, where are you when we get old? Could I just pass on without bother or prolonged care? Could I continue to work on my ziggurats? Just look at them on the shelves of my work shed.

"If I could move my work shed to the senior center. If I could live in a loft in the art center in Fenton."

"Can you afford rent there?" Warren agued.

"Can you climb the stairs?" Winnie asked.

"Isn't there an age limit?" someone asked. I think it was Winnie's husband. Whatever his name was.

"You think I'm too old for a loft?" I questioned.

I heard a noise in the kitchen. Was it Daniel trying to get back? Was it Frank rummaging for something to eat?

"There wouldn't be room for your work shed there," one of the grandchildren said.

"There're hobby rooms," Winnie corrected her daughter. "Grandma can work with her clay there."

I raged against a God who let us come to this. I will take my ziggurats and move to hell. It would be hell to be without them. I had other gods before God. He didn't like it. How could I give up my ziggurats? They were my root and stem. A flowerless stem, I saw now, but a living stalk nonetheless.

There is fire in the root. A smoldering I felt at my toes. As for Christ: I was in reaching distance, and I didn't lift my hand. I knew I wasn't doing what was required. I chose to disobey.

Where did they go? The children who had stood before me arguing. Trying out their persuasions.

Where was I now? I hardly recognized my surroundings. Maybe they had won.

Frank's Years in the Ministry

A MINISTER'S WIFE WAS a thankless job. That's how I saw it, anyway. No wonder it drove me to ziggurats. In them, I translated my uselessness into further uselessness. In my memory, there were a lot of covered dishes at church suppers—a lot of sitting still in the pew when I wanted to shove some of the congregation aside, sometimes most of them. I had to stand at the door saying "Goodbye" and "Thank you for coming" after Sunday morning services. I knew the looks of disinterest on their faces. I even made a ziggurat called *Covered Dish*. Were my ziggurats nothing more than that?

We had more friends from the university where Frank taught, or we used to.

Sometimes I still dreamed I was a minister's wife. As for that station, I had enough of that pooled anger. We left the ministry without insurance or retirement benefits. We lived on what we could with social security, the college retirement plan, and a small savings.

"You were a minister's wife, Thelma," I said. "How did you come away satisfied? Frank left the ministry with a wayward wife and an addicted son."

"Don't blame yourself for Daniel's troubles," Thelma said. "It's not your and Frank's fault. I thought there was something devious in Daniel when he was a child. Lizbet and I were talking—"

Now I felt my fury at Thelma. "You and your daughter have no right to make judgment on my children. I don't want you talking about Daniel. You can't use my children to make yours look better in comparison."

"I can say something, Eugena, and I will," Thelma said. "I've seen what Daniel did to you. He still runs your lives—even when he's dead. How many times has John driven Frank to the lawyer's? How many nights did they go over papers?"

"Don't speak to me!" I screeched in a jolt of fury. "I won't hear." Who was she to make comment on us? Let her take care of her own little humdragons. Did they even go to church?

Thelma later apologized. I apologized in return.

Our own two children, Warren and Winnie, probably didn't go to church—at least not regularly. Frank suspected this too. I heard him once say to Warren that if he didn't go to church, at least he knew where to go when he needed help.

Journal entry, December 1: *"Sustain me with cakes" (Song 2:5).*

How could a minister's wife be spiteful? Why was I arguing with myself? I was disappointed with myself, but my anger was there. All those people who came to church and gave nothing of themselves—who had an outward form of worship, who came to be seen by others, who would hardly speak to us when they saw us on the street, or only nodded in politeness. We were not included in their circle of friends. We were outsiders. Who wants a minister at your party? No, I cannot excuse my unbelief, though I have reason to. It remains solid as rock. Or if we came to someone's house, we were expected to leave early so the party could continue as a party, not Sunday school. No—that wasn't all true. At one time we had a group of friends.

Frank's Death

DANIEL WAS PLAYING IN the yard with a ball when he was a boy.

"It's all swelled up," he said of the round ball. It was an old rubber ball, a side of it pushed in. Later, the rain collected in the crumpled part. Daniel wanted something in which to collect his dreams that he could never reach. As Frank was dying, his thumb continually moved as though making an indention. He was working, working, to make a smashed-in place in a rubber ball, turning the ball into a bowl made to hold rain water.

The doctor offered to transfer Frank to Fenton's hospital, but I declined the offer. There was nothing they could do. He wanted to be in his own bed. He made that clear while he was still conscious. He didn't want his life prolonged. We had had a string of visiting nurses. He had been in assisted living. Now he was in hospice. Winnie and Warren arrived before he died.

The next morning, I sat in Frank's study, where the sunlight plowed two ruts through the window. I was waiting for the minister to arrive. I found a folder marked "The Uncollected Papers of Frank Winscott—Mainly My Journey through Faith." *What could I do? An old man with a wife faithful to me, but not to the Lord I served? Why had I married her? I had hope for her conversion. I did not realize how deep she would remain in doubt. It was her ziggurat she would travel all our married life. I battered her with the gospel. I preached to my congregation all my years, but it was Eugena to whom I addressed my sermons. If I could convert her, then my ministry would have significance. Why did some people believe and others did not, no matter how many arguments for the existence of God were placed before them? Eugena always sat on the pew with a pleasant look on her face. But what was she thinking as I delivered my well-structured sermons? Was she in her* work shed, thinking about the next ziggurat she would make? At one time, the local college asked me if she would like to teach in the art department. I said she would not. She was more interested in working with ziggurats alone in her work shed.

I let the paper fall from my lap. I could hear Frank's voice in the words I read. How could he not have asked me if I wanted to teach? Why had he made that decision for me?

I continued reading other papers. *When Daniel first came to me with his problem, I did not take him seriously. Like many young people, he'd played with drugs. Then he was supposed to pull away from them. I hoped he would go into the ministry. As a child, he seemed drawn to it. He watched me during my sermons. He would ask questions. He was converted at the altar. That was my conviction for a long time. Eugena still held that belief. It was what she said anyway, thought I knew she probably wasn't convinced. I didn't think Daniel was in heaven, though I told her I thought he was. If he was, he would have found power to overcome his trouble. Daniel made a decision as a boy, but it hadn't settled in. Why now, years later, do I doubt everything I'm saying?*

I looked up from the paper because I thought I heard a car. I listened for a moment but decided it passed and was farther away, probably turning around to try to find its way back toward Fenton.

I read Frank's papers again. *Daniel and I continued to talk in my office until our discussions turned into arguments. He could not continue with drugs. Faith would see him through. It would relieve his craving. It would lead him to the place for which he was meant. He had a sense of spiritual matters. He could have been a minister. But maybe he was—a minister of drugs. I disliked my sinister attitude at that moment, but it was Daniel's actions that were the cause. What else could I think? I grieved for Daniel. John Winscott was the staff on which I leaned through those years. John was an uncle more like a brother. He and Thelma have a son, Thomas, who worried them. But Thomas recovered, married, and held a steady job. I hoped for the same for Daniel. But he kept his mother and me in disappointment and frustration. It was the need for constant money to support his habit. I broke down before John on several occasions before his death. He simply let me cry.*

I turned through several pages until I saw my name and began reading again. *Eugena is dependent on ziggurats. There is something in ziggurats I cannot give her. A creative life she longs for. I let her go. I have to let her go. She would not survive otherwise. There is something about having a child in trouble that links her heart to his. He nearly pulled her in the grave. I think Daniel is still trying.*

There were hundreds of papers in Frank's collection. What would I do with them? Were they meant for anyone else but him? Did I want Warren and Winnie seeing them? Certainly no one outside the family. I would have to separate his private voice from the more academic voice of his translations. But often, it seemed they were intertwined. There were even letters from the lawyers mixed in with Frank's work. I tore them up in anger. Papers and papers. Whatever I did with Frank's academic work, I would have a lot of sorting to do. And did I want to do it? For what purpose?

I read another passage. *I discovered the car belonged to a man named Thomas Hopper. Daniel had a life he didn't share with me. I couldn't help the police. Hopper was a man I didn't know. He denied any knowledge of Daniel. He said he had neglected to lock the car. Daniel must have found the spare key he kept under the floor mat. The story was suspect. The investigation would continue.*

I continued reading Frank's words. *I have to keep busy while she's in the work shed, fragile as that blue scarf of her mother's she kept in her closet. I'm grateful for the distraction of translation. I have seen more than I ever imagined in the Scriptures.*

Why hadn't Frank told me about Thomas Hopper? Maybe it was to spare me further anguish. Maybe he thought it would rile me. He was right. Yes, Daniel riled me. Everything about his death riled me. His life also, for that matter. The fact that I could not know what happened, and that the police did not want to investigate, was obvious. Daniel was driving too fast on the curve and ran off the road. What else did I need to know? How cruel to live with mystery.

Winnie came into the room, and I looked up, startled. I thought for a moment it was Frank. She had just woken. Warren was still asleep. The minister would arrive. There would be a wake, the funeral, the departure of Warren and Winnie. Then?

Another Visit to the Cemetery

AFTER FRANK'S DEATH, I traveled in rings of descent. At first, they were so wide I didn't know the grading was there. But each decision took me down a path to my own invention, or intention.

What would I do with Frank's papers? His notes, his pages of writings and translations. I opened more drawers of files in his study; they were full of papers. The cabinets under his bookshelves. There were pages in the pages of his books. They looked like scarecrows. There were boxes in the attic. I was afraid to go up there because I knew it was full of papers.

Thelma wouldn't have them. "My house is full of papers also. I was thinking of asking Frank if he would take John's notes."

Our denomination has a library. The university where Frank taught? The local college where he lectured now and then? I contacted them, but they were not interested.

"I used to hear John mutter in his sleep," Thelma said. "He was still translating the Bible. He kept it all in his head. I think in his sleep, he discussed with Frank what he was thinking. Sometimes, I imagine they are still talking in the afterlife."

"Oh, don't tell me the afterlife is like it is here."

"You know it probably is."

Would Warren or Winnie want Frank's papers? Or would they come in and clean out everything? Put an industrial dumpster in the drive and pile all our belongings in it? What would they do with my work shed? Throw out my ziggurats? No—the thought was unbearable. Is that what we do? Burden our offspring with our life's work. Does it all come to rubble no one wants or knows what to do with? We leave our mess for those we leave behind—we bestow upon them what we didn't clean up.

If there was a God in heaven, all our work would be transported with us. We could continue to work forever on our projects. That's the way I wanted it. I wanted to live at least nine hundred years, then ask for more.

I could burn Frank's papers in the old incinerator in the backyard. It had been against the law to burn leaves and rubbish for years. The autumn was dry. There was dust in the wind. The burning would spark the surrounding trees. It would ignite the world.

I could set the papers out for the trash haulers, one box at a time.

I could continue to listen to the papers debate one another. Is that what those voices were in the night? And the thought that someone was coming for me. Was it the paranoia of aging? No, it was comfort. Maybe Frank would be with them. Maybe he came back to his study at night. If I went to look, he would have to leave before I saw him. I knew to stay in bed and listen to him working.

But Frank was not with them—those voices I heard in the night. That group that seemed to hover downstairs in his study. I knew no one was there. But they were.

What was it? Who were they? I didn't know them. They wanted me to come with them. No, I told them. They were not as kind as they once had been. I grew suspicious. It was too late. I couldn't go back but had to continue in the way I had planned. When had I planned this? I argued with them. They were not going to listen. I didn't want anything they offered. I felt their pecks, their scratchings. No, I didn't like this crew. They had no respect. They were just after what they wanted. I didn't trust them. Frank would not want them around me. Where was he? Had he abandoned me?

It seems everything had shifted. I was in a world of pieces, none of which fit together. How much time has passed? Was I remembering? Was I seeing what was ahead? No, there was no time here. I sat at the table eating. I sat on the edge of the bed. I walked in the hall with my walker, looking for my work shed. Who was with me? Strangers, all of them. I didn't like them. I wouldn't cooperate. I was supposed to lift my leg. Stretch my arm. Boring. Boring. I wasn't interested. Leave me alone.

"She's belligerent," I heard them say.

"Let her have her way for now," I heard another.

Wired

It was when Frank taught at a university several hundred miles from Fenton that Warren came back and lived in the house. He had just finished college. He could work online, he said. That's why our house was wired. I liked the technical images with which Warren spoke. I liked those little memories that came back, solid as ziggurats.

Warren returned to our house near Fenton several times over the years, once with a friend, saying the jobs they wanted were sitting in another country. They stayed several months, then moved on. He had long talks with Frank, which I overheard. Finally, Warren decided to return to the university where he had graduated. He wanted to study physics. There were several women who came and went with Warren. But finally one stuck, and I had a daughter-in-law, something Daniel could not provide for me. Warren continued his education until he had a PhD in physics. Eventually, there were grandchildren—Frank, Lilly. Was there no Eugena? Not that I remember. No Willoughby Winscott? But I was old, and the children were leaves running through the yard. Winnie had her hair tied back, but her children's faces were showing beneath their Winscott hair as if from a wilderness.

I'm still translating my restlessness into clay. My resistance. My uselessness. My confusion. I wish the mind were something I could trust. Sometimes I wondered if Daniel lived at all. Maybe I was hoping he would no longer seem real. No, I couldn't deny that. We'd been through a horrific time with him. What exactly had caused it?

A Sign on the Road

AFTER WORKING ALL MORNING, Frank would back the car from its garage. We started going out for burgers at noon. It bypassed some of the messiness that seemed to go with aging. I needed the long stretch of road into Fenton. I would be on a tangent—going here and there with the designs for my small clay figures. Daniel, our son, somehow entangled in my work. Then we'd drive to Fenton, and I would feel straight again. If the road curved, I curved back into my tangent.

It's why I liked the vacations that drove everyone else mad. The interstates that went on and on for miles. I could spend days crossing Kansas, Wyoming, North and South Dakota. Frank, my husband, and the children would be incensed at the thought. It was as though I knew what was ahead and tried to outrun it. I wanted the blessing of straightforward barrenness. It was a respite from my turmoil.

But the blessing of the miles eventually go by slowly. A mile is long. There was a stretch where I would say, "I can see for twenty miles," but when Frank measured it on the odometer, it was barely three.

Now that I can't go anywhere, I go over that road in my mind. They come into my room to see if I'm in place. They seem to think I'm a device that could misfire.

> Journal entry, August 8: *Where are the hills that used to be the plain where the past was?*

Those were the kinds of thoughts that wandered through my mind in wads that weren't sure where they were going. It was the kind of thinking that troubled me. It wasn't only senescence—I'd had it all my life.

"The Bible is your straight road," Frank said to me once, when I wanted to go on another long driving journey. By then the children were grown. It would have been just us—him and me. When I needed the road, sometimes he read the straight passages he found in the Bible "He leaves us a sign of his coming—a sign on the road. The powers in the heavens will be shaken" (Mark 13:25). What could be more straightforward than that? Frank asked. But what did that mean? Probably nothing, I thought. Didn't I leave a sign by the road? Did anyone stop to buy ziggurats?

The years Frank taught biblical studies at the university, either before, after, or during his ministry, he would spend hours on his syllabi. He overthought each reading for each class. Each direction for each discussion. My syllabus would be caustic. It would run the gamut of thought. No one would know where they were going, most of all me. I think in fragments and convolutions. I have a short attention span now, but one that generously goes around multiple curves. Warren, our younger son, teaches physics. He gave me the idea of a universe with multiple dimensions.

There are two hundred miles of curving road through the Bitterroots from Missoula, Montana, to Lewiston, Idaho. Was there one straight stretch? Frank and the children seemed to like it. It followed a little river. What was its name? It was the six hundred miles across Montana that drove them crazy until no amount of road games would appease their grouchiness. Their touchiness. Their whining. Daniel, Warren, and Winnie, our children. Daniel—who later drove us mad with his deaths. At least, it always seemed he died again and again.

I didn't need further diversions. There were enough of them already.

I would wake fretful. Where was I? What was happening? Who was I? Eugena Winscott. At one time, I sat in front of a congregation. At one time, a group of people came to our house on Sunday night to read *The Divine Comedy*. At one time, I had children. At one time, I spent all day in my work shed.

At first, I felt age in my left leg. It did not want to bear weight. It seemed to grow older before my right leg. When I walked, the left leg complained like a child that had been wounded in some manner. A wound that no one could see, like a scratch that would heal under a Band-Aid. It was more in the socket where my leg joined my hip. It was more of an addiction.

Senescence had an *essence* to it. There was a lilt. Lilts have been important to my work. I have mentioned my pleasure in passing over a lilting but straight road. It could rise over a hill as long as it was straight. I asked questions of my ziggurats. Could they lilt to the side of the road if they descended like the inferno? Could they lilt into the air if they ascended like Babel? Often, my ziggurats were abstract shapes. They were connotations, of course, with mysterious underpinings. They were exploration. They were a search for meaning. They were attempt. They were dislocation. They were despair. Ziggurats were a faction. A deception of memory. They were lumps with found objects sticking from them. A twig. A feather. They were shapes that used the blueness of form. They were amplitude. Ziggurats moved through time-space. Somewhere there was another plane that took other dimensions to explain, Warren had told us. Ziggurats were the black holes that connected them.

Often, I was going one way, then suddenly another way that I didn't see coming or particularly want would be there—which was Daniel's addiction inserting itself everywhere.

One evening long ago, Frank read the story of Babel to me. Then I read it myself. From the first line in Gen 11:2-8, I decided to follow it. The Bible people journeyed from the east until they found a plain. And they said, "Let's build a ziggurat whose top may reach heaven, and let's make a name, lest we be scattered over the whole earth." And they made bricks and burned them thoroughly. And the Lord came down to see the ziggurat. And the Lord said, "The people are one, and they have one language, and nothing will be withheld from them that they have imagined to do. Let us confound their language, that they may not understand one another's speech." So the Lord scattered them abroad on the earth, and they ceased building the city—and the people were scattered.

I began using the word "and" to connect long stretches of my thinking, always curving around and around into different places.

And they said.

And they went.

And they made.

My first work was bricks—to continue the work of Babel. Some of them are still along the overgrown path to my work shed behind the house. Then I began making ziggurats. One year, Frank gave me a kiln, which saved the long trip to the college in the next town.

Often my interior life was Babel. That's what I called it. "I feel like Babel," I would say to Frank in our later years, as my thoughts grew more intertwined with our yard and the field next to it. Nor could I see much difference between the yard and the garden somewhere under the weeds that covered it.

There were mornings when I think the Lord had come down to my shed to see what I was making. My worktable was disturbed. My ziggurats had been moved.

"Opossum," Frank said. "Maybe you left the door ajar, or didn't close the window. "

Daniel's drug addiction was a place hidden in him for a while. At first, I could look at him and not notice. At first, I could take a step away from that thought, if I waited a moment and let other thoughts come in. Then I began to notice Daniel's eyes. I saw the slight tremor of his hands. The sweating. The restlessness. The desperation. The horror that passed in my own mind as his addiction hardened into the ziggurat he became. I saw the folding up of the road I thought had been possible.

I felt someone breaking in—the way I feared Daniel breaking into the house—but it wasn't him. It was the voice of someone wanting to speak. To hold the road when I began to drift.

One night, Daniel came to her in a dream. He had gone off the road into a ravine and was calling her. No, he wasn't calling her. It was the drugs that had become his mother. He was only calling her to find them for him. His mother and father were a means of attaining what he wanted, and that was drugs. His parents meant nothing to him. His brother, Warren. His sister, Winnie. He wasn't even thinking of them. They had nothing he could use. They would not give him his drugs. Or means to get drugs. His mother had given him money for a while. Then she stopped. He was angry at her, and he hit her and knocked her to the floor. Afterwards, his parents filed a restraining order, and he couldn't come near their house. (Frank feared for their lives.) Was it his father who stopped her from giving Daniel the money he wanted? He wouldn't give him money any longer either. Daniel's mother sat in her work shed and made clay mounds. They went nowhere. Did nothing. What was her problem? She could do something that earned money that supplied his drugs. That was her job—to provide for him. Why did the drugs cost money? They were a product. Someone had to make them. Someone had to deliver. Give them to him. Give him. Now. Now. He needed them. Craved them. He burned for them. He was coming apart without them. He was a consuming fire. "Woe to them who build cities on blood" (Hab 2:12). Woe to them who cause blood. Woe to them. Woe. Woe. Woe. He would go to his parent's house despite the restraining order and make them get the money they had in the bank. They were saving it for him when they died, and he needed it now. It was his. He would get it. He would have his fix. Now. Now. Now. Didn't they know he had to have drugs? He would do anything for them. If only the car would go faster. He turned, and the curves on the road turned too—then a straight stretch where he could gain speed before he had to slow for the next curve on the old road north of Fenton.

Our friend Edwin Harsler liked to drive around with the mower in the back of his old pickup. He had a little ramp that lowered, and with all the pomp and lilt of an acrobat, he'd back the mower from the truck and mow the grass between the walk of the county courthouse and the curb. It was something the town mowers had already done, but sometimes in their hurry they left an uneven place. Edwin felt it needed mowed again. Or he'd find a vacant lot on the outskirts of Fenton and spend the day there. Senescence required finding something to do. The town council had a meeting and tried to stop Edwin's random mowing, but they finally decided to let him go.

"The repetition of mowing would drive me crazy," I said once at lunch when Edwin stopped by our house.

"As if spending your days in a shed with clay doesn't?" he asked in return.

I didn't want my leg replaced, though the doctor recommended it (not the leg, the hip). I would continue with it, gimped as I was, especially after standing for hours at my worktable. Frank asked if I could work sitting. Could you translate while standing? Holding all your reference books, your writing instruments, your papers? My ziggurats are an orchestra I direct. Can I do that from a chair?

This is what happens at the end of life. I wish the journey were more pleasant. But here are the words of the Lord: "When you were young, you dressed yourself and walked where you wanted; but when you are old, you stretch out your hands and another will dress you, and carry you where you don't want to go" (John 21:18).

Not the whole hip, but the ball joint—I think another doctor said. How many doctors came into the room? How many vying for the job? Upping their price at every word in a storm of forms from Medicare, other insurance papers, notices, and bills, trumped up and buffeted in our sour scouring of the government.

> Journal entry, September 18: *As if I could move all of the house. As if Edwin Harsler's mower could mow the world.*

Once you have a collapse, it's always waiting to happen again. Once you've been there, you can find your way back. Were all my children ziggurats? Had I had imagined them? The thoughts battered my head. Go with me on this journey straight west into Fenton, then north on an old curving road. If I can get the car started.

Why didn't I think of what I needed when I was there? It wasn't easy to get to the store. And when I was there, I couldn't remember what I needed. I made lists, which I also called my *syllabuses*. But they didn't seem instructive once I was in the store.

I often wrote sentences in my journal that didn't make *sense*. Another evidence of senescence. I'm only trying to find my way here.

I had a compression of bones. One bone rested on another. They continued to complain like children in the backseat of the car. I had dementia of the bones. Of the left leg and hip bone. They weren't getting along. There was no way to separate them. Did I want a cane? A walker? A hoveround? There also was the spasm of the toes when they did not want to uncurl. The spasm of my thoughts I followed in my journal, *Ziggurats and Me*.

I was a maker of ziggurats. I spent each day in my work shed. Why didn't I e-mail? Winnie called. My ziggurats piled up. They had a way of communicating. My ziggurats were my class. I heard their *sibilance*. Sometimes I knew they were humming as I approached the shed. I opened the door and they quietly looked up, as if they had not been talking at all. Ziggurats can speak without a mouth—just as there can be light without the sun.

Why is no one stopping by the house? Where are the buyers for my ziggurats? Maybe my sign was too small. I asked Edwin Harsler to enlarge the sign for me. Still no one came.

Time is lovely and convoluted. Years ago came back in an instant, while yesterday was far away, as if it happened long since. I've discovered the mind is a traitor.

Frank would leave me notes after he and his uncle John Winscott discussed *The Divine Comedy*, which they usually did on a Sunday afternoon, or evening, or all day, for that matter. No, it was a group discussion we had on Sundays after church. But Frank and John discussed it other times too. "For no other sin did I lose heaven then for not having faith," read Dante's canto 7. Sometimes I found a note in Frank's handwriting in my journal. Had he come into my shed? Did he insert the notes into the pages of my journal on their sagging shelves? Actually, there were several volumes of journals going back years.

> Journal entry, January 1: *Dante with his earflaps. I guess it was against the cold, or maybe reason itself.*

Maybe, after all, I entered oblivion to find it not oblivious, and this was my denial of it. Maybe this was Warren's version of the story, and everything was relative after all. Yes, that was the version I would tell, though another version always tried to bleed through. Is truth relative, or is truth absolute? It depends on who you ask. Warren—yes. Frank—no.

Someone at the door. They kept calling. Who was it?

"Mrs. Winscott?" Eugena heard him from her work shed. The mailman—of course. Eugena looked at him. He didn't come to the house unless he had a package.

"Is everything all right, Mrs. Winscott? Your box is full. I can't get anything into it anymore. You used to be at the box before my truck stopped. If I didn't have a letter from Winnie or Warren, I wasn't doing my job." The mailman knew when someone along his route was growing old. They paid less attention to detail. They overlooked duties they had performed faithfully for years.

From time to time, I could see things that weren't there. Shadows moved in the house. Spots crossed the dim light of the window at night—the window that looked toward the yard light, when it still worked—before the moon was darkened and the stars fell from the sky. Sometimes I would wake in another fit. Was I listening from somewhere else? Was it Daniel returned from the dead for more money to take to hell? I looked from the upstairs window to see if I saw his battered car.

More than several times, Daniel came back asking for money. In his cruelty, he hit me once on the side of my head, near my ear. For a moment I was stunned and looked cross-eyed at him and saw his two eyes as one in the middle of his face. His nose was a furious eye. Had Picasso been slapped stupid? Was that the cause of his peculiar vision of art? I wanted to make a ziggurat with one eye, but there was no worktable or kiln in an inferno, or in my interpretation of an inferno. I think that's where I was by then—which is one's judgment alone without any outside adjudication. Then I wanted to make a ziggurat that was an eye.

My hands shaped clay.

"What are you doing, Mizz Winscott?" The clouds passed the window, not looking in for once. Did you know that old ones sometimes cry out in the senior center? You can hear their cries down the halls. When I visited Frank, I recognized their cries. I think I made similar cries on my own at night in my own bed in my own house. And later, when I too was there:

"The voice of the Lord makes the hinds to calve" (Ps 29:9 KJV).

"The voice of the Lord causes the oaks to whirl" (Ps 29:9 NRSV).

"God's thunder sets the oak trees dancing" (Ps 29:9).[1]

How could the same verse have different versions? How did the translators move from deer to oaks? Maybe there was something in the original Hebrew language that meant both. But what did oaks and deer have in common? Maybe they both had antlers. It seemed no one could agree on anything. Even the same words in the same passage. No wonder Frank worked interpreting the Bible, trying to reconcile the translations. Turn it another way, and another meaning became clear. Or keep going until it translated out of its meaning. That was another issue ziggurats could explore. They walked in the margin between what was and what was thought to be.

There was a terrible winter full of snow. The oaks whirled as I walked to the road in the storm. But it was the snow whirling before the oaks that

---

1. Eugene Peterson, *THE MESSAGE: The Bible in Contemporary Language* copyright (Colorado Springs: NavPress, 2002) by.

erased their steadiness. Or moved them into the wind and the moving snow, though I believed they stayed steady on the ground—even though I couldn't see them steady—nearly disappearing in the whirling snow.

Sometimes deer came into the yard at night. I bought corn for them in the feed store in Fenton. I also fed the birds.

Journal entry, January 26: *I fought the feed store for them.*

She walked in snow to the top of her boots. But now the snow was inside her boots. Had she stepped off the drive into the narrow ditch beside the drive? Eugena felt the coldness on her legs. The wetness. Her coat unbuttoned—she pulled it close around her and fumbled with the buttons. At least she had put on her gloves. Where was her scarf? There, hanging loose around her neck. She wrapped it around her head. Why hadn't she worn her hat? Was it closer to the mailbox, or the house? Should she continue, or turn back? By the time she reached the mailbox— why had she come? Maybe there would be a letter from Warren or Winnie. Maybe there would be a letter from Daniel in hell. A missive from Frank in heaven. In the snow, divisions were erased. Yes, she could see the ground. But the air whirled like angels wings. Maybe it was the quietness of God she felt. No, he spoke in the lightning and thunder. Wasn't that what it said in the Psalms? She stopped a moment in the drive. She turned to see how far she had come from the house. Motion slows time. Those were Warren's words, her son who studied physics. How long had she been walking? It seemed a slow march to the road. She tried picking her feet up as she stepped through the snow, but quickly tired of it. She was about to give up. For a moment, she heard thunder lumbering up the road. It was Edwin Harsler.

"This course is about the process of journey," Frank would say to his class.

At first, in my *class*, I saw ziggurats from my point of view. They were my translations. Now I saw my ziggurats from their point of view. It was what they had wanted all along—to tell their own story. My work shed was, after all, their school.

"That he may set his *nest* on high" (Hab 2:9). I looked at the verse again, my glasses crooked on my face. I got my magnifying glass to sort through the words that had become clay in my hands. What would I make of them, when they could mean anything? It seems like things weren't going well for someone in the Bible—I couldn't figure out who. Someone who wasn't doing something right. "Shall they not lift up a parable against him?" (Hab 2:6). I think I was reading backwards. What would I do with these fragments? I would make ziggurats from them. A ziggurat was a parable. Frank was right. The Bible was instructive.

"It is not of the Lord of Hosts that people labor in the fire" (Hab 2:13). By then, I was reading forward again. I closed Frank's Bible, as it could be interpreted as a warning against the kiln—the firing of my clay pieces.

Frank and Warren would talk physics when Warren visited us from the university. It was no different than Frank and Uncle John Winscott talking about Scripture. Motion through space affects the passage of time. Time moved more slowly for the one moving. How could that be? I had been a young woman with children. Now I was an old woman. It seemed a swift passage, growing swifter all the time. Wasn't the whole universe gaining speed as it moved outward?

There are alternate realities—or multiple realities. Wormholes went from one point in time and space to another. I believed that. One morning as I worked in my shed, I made a ziggurat named *Worm Hole*. After I fired it, I would add it to my "Ziggurats for Sale" table, which was growing more crowded all the time.

There was someone else in the house. In my work shed, someone was writing in my journal. How many came to live with me? I ripped out their pages whenever I found them—even notes from my lovely, invisible daughter, Winnie, scared away by Daniel, who had come to her house when he saw her address on a letter she wrote. Other times, I thought it was Daniel trying to get ahold of me after his accident as he sat in his car, unable to get out—the animals prowling around him at night. Sniffing his blood. Licking his wounds. There was evidence that one of his ears had been chewed. Frank would not let me see the body, but I heard him talking to John Winscott.

> Journal entry, January 29—*Turn it inside out. Or one part of it, anyway. Or one end of it. Until there is no end of it.*

Mizz Winscott's moving her hands again. Her daughter says she's making clay. What did they think I was doing? Abstract shape is everything.

A Sign on the Road

Nothing but God could unite all forces. That was Frank's voice. It was Warren in the room with him, not John Winscott. They were arguing over multiple dimensions. Warren was pointing out something in Rev 22:2: "the tree of life was planted on either side of the river." Was there one tree or two? One, said Frank. Then how could one tree be planted in two places? How could it be on both sides of the river unless quantum mechanics were taken into consideration? Look at that verse farther down—their voices were raised now—the moment you see God, his name is on your forehead. Their discussions were a winding road that drove me crazy.

I think some mornings I saw Warren's particles with vibrating strings. If I walked outside into the bright light, my vision filled with particles of swirling snow. Not snow, of course, but visible flecks I could see. I felt them stretch and wiggle.

It wasn't Edwin Harsler who found Eugena in the snow that day, but Roland Muskee, the new minister. He had tried to call, but the phone didn't seem to be working. He had finally driven to the Winscotts' place to talk to Eugena, but he saw she was confused. He didn't correct her when she talked to him like he was someone else. He helped her into his car and drove up the drive back toward the house, skidding once in a while, but with a slow, steady hand on the wheel, he made it to the top of the drive. Eugena held a wad of mail in her hand. Roland parked beside the house and took her arm as she got out of his car. He followed her to the door, but it was locked. He saw the tracks in the snow from the side of the house to the drive and suggested they try the back door. That was where she had left the house. He tried to tell her she should be careful. He wondered if she could have walked back up the drive in the snow. Inside the house, he saw how disheveled it was. He felt the cold.

"Where's your thermostat?" he asked, looking along the walls. "Does your furnace work?" Finally, he found the knob and turned it up. After a few moments, he heard a growling from below, and the furnace belched on. Roland Muskee introduced himself, but Eugena kept talking to him as though he were Edwin Harsler.

"How's Helen?" she asked. Roland had come to the house to see about Frank's papers. It had come to him through one of the parishioners whose parents had come to the Winscotts' house for the Sunday readings of *The Divine Comedy* that Frank had a library. Roland wanted to know about the study group. He was curious about his library. He wanted to speak to the widow about donating some of the books to the church. Maybe the papers. But he found a confused old woman. He returned to the church and called the authorities. Then he called Eugena's children. The next day, Eugena was moved to the senior center in Fenton.

"Nyland," I heard Warren say to someone. Was one of my grandchildren Nyland? Wasn't that my name before marriage? Wasn't it Warren's name? Warren Nyland Winscott? Maybe it was Winnie's boy. I thought of a grandchild named Nyland. I hoped Winnie had married a man with the last name of Norris.

Those people were in the room again. Was it another meeting at our house? There was Frank sitting in his chair, smiling, ready to bring us all to order. Then he was gone. I called his name, but he didn't return. Someone was holding my arm. Let go. Let go. I want to know where Frank had gone. The meeting can't start without him.

If Eugena could drive the car again . . . If she could just reach Daniel. It was Eugena in the old car. Turning and turning the key. Waiting. Turning the key again. It was Eugena turning around in the yard. Bumping something. What a loud clunk such slow movement made. They would think someone was after him. It was drugs with visible wheels pushing him fast and faster to get to his parents, who he would make give him drugs. But he ran into a ravine where he remained for several days, dying somewhere between the wreck and the discovery of his body.

A Sign on the Road

Sometimes I crumpled a ziggurat, then uncrumpled it, as if it were Daniel's car before it went into the ravine on a curving road and hit a tree. Sometimes I stood absolutely still in my work shed and drove a straight road to the whirling, unwinding universe, where I listened to the slow dissolution of the world.

In Hell There Is No Night

SOMEWHERE, LIFE FELL AWAY, one chunk at a time, though I tried to keep it.

"No one knows what it's like," I said to Reverend Muskee.

I remembered Winnie's eventual marriage and my grandchildren, but by then I was too old to recognize them when they came for a visit. No, I remember the grandchildren. It was when they were older that I had trouble remembering who they were. Warren was also married. I don't remember which one of them married first. Maybe they overlapped. What was my daughter-in-law's name? My son-in-law, for that matter? Grant, I think. Somewhere, Edwin Harsler died. I remember Helen's face pushed close to mine.

"Hello Eugena, it's Helen," she insisted. Then she was telling someone else. Gradually, I lost my independence—my ability to care for myself. Finally, my desire to work with clay.

"In the end, it is that core of eternal life given us when we accepted Christ as our savior," Frank said before his death. "Take it Eugena," he pleaded, but it was a place I could not reach. I had a life I had to live as a clown. Yes, ziggurats were my costume.

I just didn't understand how anyone could go to hell, unless they were Hitler or the torturers of the world.

Once, Frank was reading in the chair while I unpacked our suitcases after one of our trips. I think the children were scuffling, and he had gone to see what the matter was. I heard him use Scripture on them, and the fighting ceased. How did that work? Frank could ameliorate their anger with a few words.

Once, I woke with my head full of ideas. Now I wake facing the North Sea again—wherever it is. Now I wake not knowing where I am. No, I know where I am—a place where I've never been. I do not want to be where I am. It is barren, if an ocean could be called barren. Lights go out on the ocean when the sun goes down, except for the stars and moon.

> Journal entry, March 17—*Terror, interesting in its garishness. Magnificent in isolation.*

Where were Frank's "preachings of the morning" at the breakfast table?

At one time I had canned vegetables from the garden. There was a crooked little pear tree by my work shed. The pears were too hard and bitter to eat, but I pulverized them with my meat cleaver. I drowned them in sugar. Frank could tolerate one teaspoon of my pear puree on his salad. Or if I baked a pie, he would eat the crust.

How far away Frank's words now seemed. Did I make note of them to use them in my ziggurats? Did I want to see how I could turn them upside-down into something I wanted to hear?

Christianity. Much had been made over it because we needed a structure of some sort on which to hang the sorrows of our lives. To justify the struggle. To maintain a sense of justice somewhere in the universe. To know there was a God that someone would have to stand before and answer to.

But weren't the Christians persecuted? Wasn't the Apostle Paul driven from town to town when he preached? Jesus lived and died as Frank said, and afterwards, his followers were jailed, stoned, tarred and feathered, beheaded, crucified upside-down. "Get those Christians out of here. Shut them up. That is the common reaction to your story, Frank," I said, though I knew he was absent at the moment. We want directives, yet end up fleeing what we're told. We strive for order, yet we leave upheaval in our wake. We live together, it seems for all our lives, yet we die far apart.

Where was the paper I wanted? Why couldn't I find the earlier *Ziggurat Journals*? What happened to them? What were all these loose papers before me? Why didn't I make notations of the year of the journal entries? They rotated like the earth around the sun without attention to which year the journey had been made. They all blurred together as if the years were dyes that seeped into one another. Or rain on the newspaper until the words ran together? Why didn't I listen to what the Scriptures said?

I felt them all fade from me as I floated into a dark place full of heat.

In hell, we could not understand one another. That's the first thing I can say. I could tell what they were saying was language, but it was not words I could understand. Shame and embarrassment was there. The loneliness without language. We turned away from each other. It was the only thing we could do.

Sometimes Frank's words would come back. It was like I was hearing him speak somewhere without seeing him. "She made nothing functional," he said. "Nothing of use." It was like the language of hell: *She's out there slapping clay on the table, but there will be no pot from which to pour tea. No bowl in which apples can sit. No plate for a piece of bread.* I saw the branches of several trees through a window. It was as if the pages of our journals were pasted together. *Her work is to show us a way to see.*

I know it isn't ziggurats that God likes. I could tell by the look on other people's faces. But I held the ziggurats up to God in my self-will. My worship was the time I spent alone with my work. Ziggurats were not without recognition, I decided. The ziggurats were my thoughts. What did I think? Hell is a place where no one listens. Maybe they listen, but they don't hear. That is the story of ziggurats. They are the separation from God. They are a matter of perception, or an assumption about the world on one's own terms. Frank's idea of heaven must have been close. I could hear them, far off in the distance.

His objection—ziggurats were the work of my own hand.

Fragments Came to Me and Patterned Themselves as Ziggurats

Don't let her go to hell. She's a potter.
—ANNE KINGSBURY

I found it marvelously dark.
—DANTE, *THE DIVINE COMEDY*, CANTO 21

WHAT IS IT LIKE to die? I expected sleep. I expected forgetfulness. I expected oblivion—except for my ziggurats, which would bear witness to my having been on earth. I was afraid of the passage, of course. No one tells us about it, but when the time came, I felt a rise and fall—the way it felt in the backseat of the car when Edwin Harsler drove over the crest of a hill and the car started its descent. I actually wondered if I had died. It was God's revenge all over again. After death, I am still alive in a dwarfy sort of place. Dark and funky. A place of small tortures.

One day the dark one, the escort in hell (where I chose to be by my own actions) was listening to the noise from heaven, as I was. That was another torture here—we could hear the praises in heaven. All the little tears wiped away, all the squeaky voices singing to God on the other side. I cannot trust where I am. You shouldn't worry as you read this. It may not be correct. Or true. If there is a difference. I am a haunted old woman full of memories that clunk like ziggurats when I pushed them off the table. Did I ever make ziggurats? Yes, I think I did. I put one on Frank's grave. One on Uncle John Winscott's. One on Edna Woodruff's. One on Daniel's. I'm sure I made the ziggurats. I put them on other graves—those who never bought them when they were alive. Until the caretaker stopped me. "Mrs. Winscott, get ahold of yourself," I remember someone saying. What a dizzying place. Who else was there to take me away?

I think now this is my madness showing, though I don't believe I'm mad. Hell is imagination. If only there was oblivion, I would be happy. I would gladly report it.

"They're at it again out there," I heard someone's voice. The voices came across the great chasm from heaven. But there was no praising here. Here there was darkness—the air has the smell of an oil spill. It is a black sluggishness someone called a lake. The oil spill happened to show us this aspect of hell, but did we learn? Other than the sight of seagulls clogged with oiled wings stuck to their sides.

Where is a scarf to wipe my sweat?

Where is a clown to lighten my load?

In hell, there is no night. Fire, yes. But it is dark, mostly dark—a dark you can touch. There's no sleep. And no dream. It is a crazy nightmare. That's what hell is. A nightmare prepared by one's own mind from which there is no waking, though I am awake inside it—without the leveling and correction of the Holy Spirit, Frank would say. I wish he were here to lecture me. After seeing this place, I might listen.

Yes, hell is the darkness of a musty, red-orange glow. It's an immense cavern, unimaginable in size, full of the smell of fire. When I was a child, we returned from my grandparents' farm with the stink of smoke from the woodstove. Sometimes I think we're still on the farm, though I know we are not. In hell, people argue with themselves. I hear something like the noises I remembered between my mother and father.

Sometimes a red moon comes up over the rim of hell. Those farther down in the ziggurat cannot see it, but the message is passed down and down where the passage grows smaller and hotter. The people form a dry, restless, moving, troubled, heated sea. I'm not sure anyone cares.

Though I didn't know where he was, I send the message of the moon to Daniel, hoping it arrived, but knowing no one was interested in passing a message along. Absolute self-absorption is the attitude of hell.

Fragments Came to Me and Patterned Themselves as Ziggurats

I felt the dark one move closer. At one time, when I was still in *life*, there was someone else—a more benevolent being who attended me. But I must have let it go. I must have said, "Your services are no longer needed." Now there was a dark one. It was the strange presence I had felt in the room of my madness.

How long do we translate and understand nothing?

———•-•———

I have been looking for Daniel in hell, though we don't get too far away from ourselves. The roads are slogged, and it's hard to travel. They're muddy as the old road to my grandparents' farm. Once a tractor had to pull our car through the mud when my father got stuck. But here there are no tractors. I try to keep the thought of my own death stored in a box, folding the flaps on top over one another. But somehow they kept getting loose.

One night in hell, or maybe it was day—I was trying to scrape the mud from my legs, but I saw it wasn't actually mud, but some viscous material, thick and slumpy. I wondered if it could be used for ziggurats, but there was no making of anything here.

I wanted to make ziggurats to describe the self in its wretched descent into itself. Hell is a place full of the art of one's own making. After all, ziggurats were a world of my own making. A thought of the Guggenheim Museum zipped through my head. Upside-down. Yet above-ground in New York City. A ziggurat is attitude. I could believe I was an artificer when I worked with the circles within. I worked with that concept all my life. Hell was a longing for work. I still have flashes of my beloved ziggurats. I still imagine I work. This ziggurat looks like the blueprint for an ark, one story on top of another. Another ziggurat looks like a military tank.

———•-•———

There are cold spots in hell—they are the mountains of regret. That's the first thing I learned. You don't argue for your innocence. Secondly, you don't doubt the reality of hell. It is here for the one who based herself in her own accomplishments, who ignored the lightings of God. But strangely, it was a place I already knew. I knew it was where I belonged.

Then there are those who walked off with other people's money. There are murderers. Betrayers. But it wasn't what got them here. It was the lack of faith in Christ. That's what I see from my realm of hell. The worse ones are lower down. The ones with minimal flaws are higher up. But they are all here—in the ziggurat of hell.

What is it I can say to them? Sitting on the rim of this enormous furnace, one afternoon—though it could have been night or morning, for all I knew—there were no changes in time that I could tell. It was time, or the absence of time. But one afternoon, I slipped from the rim and my fingers made tire marks in the slog. I slid down a narrow, winding road for a long time. There were thick branches in the way that were not trees.

And there was Daniel, dear Daniel. He didn't know I was there. I wanted to run to him, see him healed of his drugs, but he was not. I saw he still hungered for what was not available. He tried to lap up the sludge that surrounded him. One ear bent to the side. He moved slug-like as he crawled along the ground. Was he still paralyzed? My heart sank the moment I could concentrate on him—before I returned to my own hell of self-absorption. We can only go so far, and no farther into hell. Did I see him with a telescope? I didn't know. Distance seemed screwed into place. But I felt I should be there with him. Like the mother who entered the gas chambers in WWII Germany so that her crippled son would not have to go alone. But this chamber was different. We survived our gassing. We were locked in a place from which there was no release. Gassed every day. Every day dying to what we were. There was no dawn for us.

I tried to talk to Daniel, but he seemed only to hear himself. The awful grieving of it was there. The sorrow that this was my son forever. It was a grief that opened and opened without end. "*Should I hide my new radio? Where is my mother's silver?*" The grief had petals of anger opening from it. It streaked us with a dull red glare. But I have no radio or silver. We have nothing with us here but the belongings of our thoughts. The furniture of our head.

"*What happened on the road? Who was that man I saw? Did you know that woman at your funeral? That man?*" There it was again—the mystery of Daniel's death held out to me. The ruts that haunted. Would I ever know? Was that my punishment? One of my punishments?

Daniel looked up a moment as though recognizing someone was addressing him, but his misery was a shield to anyone beyond himself. How could God leave us with our questions unanswered? Daniel was my own child, and I could not know?

Fragments Came to Me and Patterned Themselves as Ziggurats

"*Are you deaf?*" I shouted to him. "*This is forever!*" I don't think God heard. I don't think Daniel even saw me, though he turned his head again. His face was somewhat covered by his usual mop of hair. I had the horrid thought that maybe he had no eyes. Maybe he had paid for drugs with them.

I turned from the horror that was Daniel. There were shadows over there. Where are they now? When I looked back, I was separated from Daniel again. He seemed to sink back into the mire. The burning was still here. I had not moved. But there were new shadows. New turnings. I could not dispel the thought that somewhere the season had changed. Yet the same molasses of darkness covered everywhere I looked. Kudzu came to mind, then floated away.

Far away, something was happening.

A new growling. Someone had been let into the lower ring. I knew it then. I lived in a ziggurat all my life. I had been working with the form I would inhabit forever. I could not bear the thought of forever. It was horrific. But I knew this was where I would be. It was more of a canyon, circling downward. Had we ever taken a mule down the trail at the Grand Canyon? Had Frank and the children and I been there? I don't think so—but I knew memory was unstable. I couldn't always count on the truth of what I thought. I argued with myself.

Whoever had been let into hell was angry. I held my hand to my ears because of the roaring. I wanted to find Daniel to cover his ears. To hide him from further suffering or fear, but I could not find him. Maybe it was my own madness I was hearing. *Shut up down there!*

It was someone who had done a great evil. Someone who didn't know he wouldn't rule in the life after death. Someone who had never given Christ a thought. Someone who didn't know there was a God who would reject him from the world he expected.

There was a banging of chains for a long time. There was a challenge. To live with this. It isn't what I wanted.

Daniel never came to see me. I think he knew I was there. You know, in hell, who is there. And who is not. I wanted to get back to Warren and Winnie, who were still alive. I wanted to tell them, beware. But there was no mail service. No Internet. There was no phone, though I often felt for the cell phone they gave me. I never could find it. I thought I had brought it with me. Did all disappear here? Did it play tricks? What kind of landscape was this? Who designed it? Who was the planner of the afterlife? They needed a few lessons. They should have studied architecture. City planning. Avenues with trees.

Was this a quarry? A sulfur mine? Galactic in size. We were miners trapped below. I heard them cry for a while, but then they had no more water for their tears. They learned to suck it up.

I bear the mark of the fugitive I carried all my life.

It was all that talk I should have listened to. Why wasn't Frank more explicit? Why didn't he say, "Do you want to spend forever in hell, Eugena?" What would I have said? No, of course, not Frank, but all roads lead to the same God. But where was he? Not present. Absent that day. I wanted to talk to him. What was the matter? I should call his house and see if he's all right. How could something I dismissed be the border between this difference?

I got tired of my feet being globbed with mud. I slipped again on an incline, my two fingers drawing more tracks in the sludge, trying to grip the edge. Was it the witness of another car on the road behind Daniel's? Had he been pushed after all? Would I have this mystery repeating itself forever, going around and around in my head without answer?

The miners in Chile could not sleep after they came up from the mines because they had been terrorized. They had been in hell. They still carried with them their pick and shovel, digging their way out.

Hell is a continual distress. It is unrest. It is a feeling of doom. A continual unsatisfied longing. A frantic fretfulness. A deep and abiding fear.

What I miss now is a bathtub.

I remembered when Frank slept beside me with the rhythmic snoring of someone going far away. He was a train in the distance. A steamer down some wide river through a distant land. A land into which I could not go.

This mystery of sleep. Of reservoir. Of reserve. Of rejection. I felt that language had rejected us. That it went off to be what it was without us. In the end, I knew language was God. Or at least an aspect of Christ: "In the beginning was the Word." That, you see, was where my husband went in his heaven—into the space of language.

Fragments Came to Me and Patterned Themselves as Ziggurats

At night, there was a rowing of a boat upriver. In his breathing, I could hear the air at war with its passage into his lungs. It was memory that was almost real.

There was narrative in abstraction. Abstraction formed in the narrative, and the narrative formed in the abstract. It was a thought I carried in my ziggurats. The ironic witness testifying what I didn't want it to testify.

When Daniel turned to his internal world and did not care about his surroundings, I saw his descent into hell before it actually happened. When had I first seen it, and refused to recognize the danger? What could I have done? Drugs were his god, and he worshipped daily. He had a strange intensity, even as a child. An inability to join in. An irascibility. A stealthiness. Was I seeing myself? Was Daniel a part of me? Was I still making excuses? Somewhere, the dark one came for him, and he went with him. Daniel had no choice. No, his choice had been drugs. *It's not my fault!*

It was the heat. The heat and the heat. The unrelenting summers. I had tried to use a fan in the work shed, but it dried the clay too soon. Finally, I had an old buzzing air conditioner Edwin Harsler helped Frank install.

Black energy. Bat energy. Black holes. Each rung of hell sits on one of them.

A verse that Frank used on me comes back now and then. Luke 16:19–31, Lazarus and the rich man. I think of Lazarus the beggar in the chorus of praise I can hear from heaven. Sometimes, I think I hear Frank's voice when the rejoicing becomes overjoyed. I see him standing at the pulpit in his ministerial robe. There were times in church when Frank's voice would lift above the hymn. There always was a certain note where his voice stood out. Then I had the thought—the rich man was in hell. In Scripture, he could hear the beggar sing. Was the rich man here? Had I passed him on the way to find Daniel?

I felt at times I could step onto the larger rim of heaven, but I was afraid I would slide down farther into hell. I held to my ledge until my fingers ached, or slipped to make tire tracks again.

My hope in a lie was my truth here. Hell was like the fiery furnace in which Daniel's friends walked but were not consumed. The Daniel in the Bible—Shadrach. Meshach. Abednego. I'm sure our son's friends were in hell with him.

I remembered a quote I wrote on a ziggurat: "because he gave fraudulent counsel since which I have kept fast by his hair" in canto 17 of Dante's *Inferno*.

No, it is the thought of Daniel that sticks to my hair.

I try to push him away into the sludge in hell, but it is caked. What color this air? Something like the oxblood I once used for a ziggurat.

There were others I almost knew but could not quite recognize. I lived in a dim haze, unfulfilled, with nothing to accomplish, nothing to know but my own thoughts. Was this hell? Is this what was ahead of me forever?

What did Winnie and Warren do with my ziggurats after my death? Did they set them out beside the road? Was the whole house slowly decaying like those old abandoned houses I saw, ready to collapse? Did Warren and Winnie throw my ziggurats out on the edge of the field to become earth again? Earth to earth—where they became a rock city. Did they give them away at my funeral? And who preached my funeral? What was that minister's name at our church? Maybe I should have listened, but I think I worked with an inferno all my life and never knew it.

As I sit here on the upper rim. No lightings anywhere.

How Could A Minister's Wife Be Found in Hell?

I ALMOST MADE IT into heaven. I almost believed, but I sidestepped it in the end out of stubbornness and hurt and defiance.

Frank was right. We don't visit with each other in this place. We are locked in our own head. I could view Daniel if I made a long trip through a sloggy road. But not to visit.

I do have memory from time to time. I see the loveliness of the work with my ziggurats to hide the evil beneath. What was my evil? I tried to shape God with my own hands.

Once I had lived in the middle of Frank's words that would have been islands, but I preferred drowning. I didn't want Christianity.

I can pass where I want now, after being bedfast. Some of the vapor trails must be mine. No, I think now they were Frank's.

What do we do with this bully—drugs? Or drug use. If drugs were left on the shelf, what would it matter? Daniel told us they were everywhere. When you don't take drugs, you don't know them, but when you do, you see them everywhere. I could have a stash of cocaine or meth or any of the drugs I didn't know the name of on my breakfast table, and it would sit there before Frank forever without the slightest temptation, because we hadn't grooved it into our minds.

I'm in the same place as Daniel, but it's not the comfort I expected. I don't see him. Often now, I'm not very interested in seeing him. How cruel hell is—little snatches of life come back, but just as you think you have them they zip off, and you're locked into yourself again.

Where is truth? Revelation? They are not here either.

If I didn't know the truth, I would invent it. The whole earth had been one language, but now it was many, so I could tell my own story. It didn't matter what other languages and other versions were. I could make up my own.

In my imagination, I wrote, *The Journal of Daniel Winscott*: *Daniel had ridden with a man named Hopper—Jack Hopper, I think was his name. No, Thomas Hopper. To a meeting north of Fenton where Daniel had a meeting to be healed. In the meeting, Daniel was healed. Thomas Hopper loaned Daniel his car to drive to our place to tell us because his cell phone wasn't working. It hadn't worked because he had dropped in a lake by mistake. It was on the road—someone appeared in the air, and Daniel reached up to him and left this earth.* I had known that already. Or suspicioned it. The car was not stolen. It was loaned. But why was Daniel taken once he was healed? Was it merely an accident? Accidents did happen. Accidents were their own hell in themselves. What goofiness was I perpetrating on myself? No, it made sense. What was a car but a clown suit we ride to hell?

Far

Be strong, yes, be strong.

—Dan 10:19

Once in a while in the distance, I can hear across the galaxies to the ball of grace I had been told about in life but had not accepted. I sat in church for years, and that alone was not acceptable to the Beloved? I had notches on my belt for each sermon I had heard. But I had to find truth for myself. What was wrong with that? In the meantime, I had polluted and ignored and made a clown suit of Frank's sermons for myself.

Maybe I had entered oblivion, and this is Frank's version of our story, and everything is relative after all. Both are true. His and mine. Husband and wife. What if everything is relative? Yes, I had argued that. It was the version I would tell.

Somewhere Frank and Uncle John were talking. Festus, the governor of what? Judea? No, Samaria—I never got those places straight—once said that Jesus was dead (Acts 25:19), and that was truth to Festus. Some believed and some did not. Maybe Festus was in hell with me. Maybe he was one of the crusted and uncommunicative miseries I passed on my way to Daniel.

At one time, I suppose I wanted Daniel gone. I wanted the gravel under him to open its mouth and swallow him and his household of drug users and family torturers so they and all that belonged to them went down alive into Sheol, and the earth closed over them, and they perished from the face of the earth.

Where did that bitterness come from? Was there nothing here to temper it? Was there nothing left in my head that would help me crawl away from my thinking?

It was all tenuous. There was unfinished business running all over the place as darkness set in. A place only a man could make. I ducked as another bat flew over my head. For supper, I ate the anger and frustration of my answered questions.

"Who is that howling?" I asked.

"It's you, Eugena," the voice said.

My thoughts gnawed my head. I could feel their teeth. I wanted to howl with the others. I can't believe there is a hell. I don't believe there is a hell. It's just imagination. But there in the rubble are painful, sordid memories with long thorns on an overgrown tree. The thought of Daniel came up. He stood in front of me as a child with a handprint of clay he had made in kindergarten—holding it up to me, his wild hair pressed to one side from sleeping on it the wrong way or from wearing a cap without smoothing his hair to the side like I told him. It was a little lump of clay—probably his teacher had flattened it for him before he pressed his open palm onto it. Was it then fired? Or was it the kind of clay that dried by itself? How long had it dried before it painted it in a garish blue? Where was it now? Lost in the rubble of my house. Lost among the ziggurats of my own work. Was it Daniel who gave me the gift of ziggurats? Was it Daniel who handed me my ziggurats—the work of my life?

Daniel in Hell

Another had his throat pierced through, and nose cut off to the eyebrows, and one single ear.

—Dante, *The Divine Comedy*, canto 28

These thoughts pass through my head like hits—they are torments that batter my brain. They are waves on an endless sea. But there is no water here. There is sludge stuck to my feet. I can't move. Dark ones sweep past me. Could they stop to talk? I reach out to them, but they are gone. No one is there. Who knew what was here? I'm blind and cannot see. But smell it I can. The suck-hole where I stand. Little snakes or lizards dart here and there.

I can't get out, but I can hear. Winnie crying about her watch. These thoughts smear my head—they can get her another one. Maybe she lost the watch, I say. Let them blame her—HA HA. Is it my laugh that is howling? What ears are these that reek with sound? What do I hear? Who are they that slither around me? I want them to go away! They swell with their own frenzy

Where my friends? We nerked about everything. We were high as wind. As kites on a black-tongued wind. Whooo. Whooo. Shut up! Stop the crying. There's one tumbling. Where'd he go?

Someone else coming around. I feel her here. What's she looking at? Go away. No business for you here. What does she know? Not this high road. Har. Those old women lamboozing in the kitchen. What would they do with it? Nothing. They're boiling potatoes. Those old women need a hit. They need to find the roof. Woof. Woof. I get blamed for everything lost or misplaced. Might as well take it. *Get away!* Think to the eff. What turns do they know? No, they'd never be ready for this. Why this stuff costs? Take another watch? Now Winnie's screaming in her room.

Who is taunting? Go away. Can pass drugs? All the names they've got for them. Whoppers take you. Consume until you are them. Don't speak. Someone might hear. Who is following? Put it here. Just know I took. What's that ticking? A watch in hell? Shove it away. It comes back. They just gave it to her. And it was gone. She didn't need to know. Who is hearing this? Crying. Crying. Why can't I see? Pitch black as the tar bucket Harsler used to try to fix the roof. I hear Helen in the field. What a slump comes over me. I chase her in the tall weeds. She screams. Now eat watch? Swallow? Now choke on it. The endless craving.

A motor running somewhere. Turn it off. Can't reach. Arm stuck to body. When I move pain eats. Here fork. Knife. The clanking silverware I took. What are they coming for? Dark figures. Go away. I'm not going. They stand by trees. Talking in the dark. Shut up. They can't get me. I'm sweating. *Mama!* Daddy! Get me here. The figures pull me out of the broken car. No one hears. I'm not yelling on earth anymore.

Any way out? No—this way forever. Where is dinner on Eugena's table? Frank reading the Bible to us? Where is a drink of water? There's the hose in the yard. I could pick it up and drink. Squirt Warren and he runs screaming to Mama—*ha ha!*

They told me stop but I didn't. The Monster got me. Those names in my ears. Horse. Hardball. Water. Where's water? *Water!* Bring drink. *Tongue hanging.* Fill mouth. *Can't breathe.* Monster pulls into chute. Black air. *Where's Frank's study light I took?* Turn it on. *Can't find. What's this place?* Darkness. Crying *darkness.* A funnel with a long trail. Where's light? Ticking down. Ticking. *A thousand years of ticking.* Batter *batter* my brain. Where's the door? *Get me out!* I'm to my chest. *Yeek.* What's rising out of my head? Stop these thoughts running into one another. These engines quiver. *Furies* run my brain. These lizards running are my fingers.

Ziggurats for Sale

THEY ARE AT OUR graves—Winnie and Warren. Not at the same time, but I feel a nick when they are there. Why do they visit? Do they think I have anything to do with the cemetery? Yet they stand at the graves of Frank and Eugena Winscott—a drone and a crone. There they are again. Again they are there. Maybe they're visiting Frank's grave, thinking of heaven with its heavenly gates and heavenly sky and whole heavenly city. The landscape of hell is at least interesting. Is there a landscape at all? There is no making here. No journals. No *Ziggurats and Me*. Just barren hotness. Darkness. Blankness. Smokiness. The torment of being locked in one's own thoughts. That's the droning here—not Frank's insistence on the Bible—but a buzzing that does not go away.

There're other voices tearing into the fabric of what I know. I swat them. They try to bury me in their vespine ways. If there's one thing here, it is wasps. Shooting around the head. Buzzing endlessly. The drones of hell. Operated somehow remotely. There's the devil with his engine room—himself tormented, tormenting others. Maybe Warren and Winnie were at our house near Fenton to disperse goods. Is Edwin Harsler still there? He would love going through our things.

Maybe the Figgetts from the art gallery in Fenton—the Art and Cultural Center—to see what could be salvaged from my work. Maybe they will get an industrial dumpster. Have a yard sale.

Frank and Uncle John Winscott must be talking away with others in the libraries of heaven. They're probably sitting in the lecture hall going over the history of the ages, the ages before the ages, and the destination of an expanding universe.

The ascent and descent of man.

The holy engineering into the Bible of what we needed to know. Leaving all the rest out. For later. If later never came, we had all we needed to know in the Bible. But later came. Later.

Graveyards always bothered me. I could feel the voices there.

There was another funeral. Thelma's? Lizbet and Winnie were there. John II, Thomas, and Warren. Look how Warren has aged. What's bothering him? Is his job difficult? Are there problems in his marriage? His children?

I could start over. The little ziggurats have other voices in my memory.

Winnie had told me about her husband, Grant. About the chance she was taking. He'd been from a family that wanted for little. But they were strange. She had decided against Grant several times, but he kept returning to her thoughts. She was getting older. Who else was pursuing her? Who else even seemed interested? Should she take what she could get? Could she live single for longer? She had a job. She could nearly support herself. Frank would send her money when she seemed to need it. How did he know? Surely we left them a little when we died. Winnie could get along by herself. She was not as independent as Helen Harsler and her high-end retail, but she managed. Did Winnie realize her parents lived in different worlds? Yet we had been happy together. We were one. She couldn't think of us separately—in separate places. What was there about the single life that charmed her? Nothing, probably, except the time she had on her own to do what she wanted.

Winnie liked Grant's sisters. She wanted to be in a family. She married him. She continued to work to have something to do. Eventually the children came. Then she began to grow concerned about her parents. She went to Fenton often. Her children stayed with her sisters-in-law. They played with their cousins. They didn't seem to mind that their mother had to go to her parents' house again—to see to their needs. To worry about what would happen to them. To fill out medical forms and pay bills. To see to details. To decide what to do with the immense work of clearing out the house where they had lived most of their lives. No updating. In disrepair. How could they sell it? Winnie asked a realtor to visit the place.

"You could sell it as-is. You could spend money to re-wire and replace the plumbing. You'll find more problems than you know are there. Then there's the shed behind the house. It would have to be torn down. It's leaning as it is. The garage door is crooked on its track. The house needs re-roofed. Re-guttered. It needs a new furnace and hot water heater. Windows need to be replaced. The house should be gutted, actually," the agent said. "What's that in the shed?"

"My mother's workshop where she made ziggurats," Winnie answered.

The agent seemed to understand that it was better not to keep asking questions. "I would suggest you and your brother take whatever you want—furniture, photo albums, books, whatever. Then have a yard sale with whatever is salable. Sometimes an auctioneer will handle the sale. There are people who buy the estate and haul it all off. If you have time, stay here and do it yourself. Finally, there's the sale of the property itself. It may be disappointing. The land is the most valuable part of the property. A nice distance from Fenton. A developer might be interested. Or someone who refurbishes houses. The house needs painting inside and out. New bathrooms and kitchen. It will probably have to be treated for termites. I don't think anyone could live in the house the way it stands now. The cost of repairs will be prohibitive, but if you don't, the house won't sell for anything."

Winnie e-mailed Warren about her conversation with the agent and the immense amount of work their parents had left them. Should they hire someone to clear it out?

She eventually called Warren because he wasn't forthcoming with many answers. "The house and garage are salvageable," she said. "Too bad Edwin Harsler isn't alive."

"He couldn't do the work," Warren interrupted. "He would just shuffle everything around and think he'd done some work. Mainly he would nose through our father's papers." Warren paused a moment. "Take the clothing to Goodwill. Call the Salvation Army to come in their truck and take what they want."

Ironic Witness

"What do you want, Warren? Dad's tiepins and cuff links? Maybe a few books? Just to keep on the bookshelf in your house. Nobody wants old books. That's most of Dad's possessions. The new minister came and asked for some of them—books and a few papers. I'll gather up the rest of Dad's writings and keep them stored in my garage for a while in case anyone thinks he might have left something important. Lizbet is here too, trying to clear out her parents' things."

Grant, it turned out, was not a good risk. Winnie had known that. Now he was taking risks that did not pay off. He and a friend started a business that didn't go anywhere. He joined a tax firm and worked there for a while, but after the busy season, he began to drift. He worked in sales for two months before he came home announcing he had quit his job. Grant could do accounting for small businesses from his house. Grant could work from home. This was during the time that Winnie had to travel to Fenton to help her parents, especially her mother. She was glad to be gone from one mess into another. Yet she only moved from one unsettledness to another, from one place where she felt she didn't belong into another. But there was work to be done at her parent's house—there was work she didn't know how to do. Why were the jobs no one wanted to do left to women? No, that wasn't true, she decided.

The first night Winnie slept in her girlhood bedroom, she covered her nose with the sheet she had washed at the laundromat in Fenton. The stale smell of the room, of the house, crept into her. The pillow was stale. The rug was musty.

One night Winnie sat before her father's large bookcases in his study. He'd spent his life with these books. She took them off the shelf and put them back, sneezing from the dust. Had her mother never cleaned? Had Mrs. Woodruff never dusted when she came to the house to clean? The books were dirty with the dust of several years. Mrs. Woodruff must have just been in the house to clean without cleaning. She must have been the recipient of her parents' charity.

Ziggurats for Sale

Winnie looked through her father's books. He'd been a theologian. That world had been something she knew was there but had never paid attention to. Even in church while her father preached, she could think of other things. She could hear her father's words and know there was a God that loved them—that ruled the world as a grand master—and she could leave all the administration to God and her father. She was free to do what she wanted. She remembered that her father had said that people had been granted free will. But she had to re-establish what her brother Daniel had left in ruin. She would not cause that suffering to her parents. She would not be an embarrassment. She would not leave her siblings with lawsuits still pending. Everyone in Fenton knew about Daniel. Everyone tried to act like he wasn't a Winscott. How could he be? The son of a minister and biblical scholar. The son of a zigguratist. Her parents and Edwin Harsler and Edna Woodruff and Uncle John Winscott and Aunt Thelma and her cousins floated like balloons into the atmosphere.

She was the offspring of parents with a lively world. Where was her lively world? Winnie had a husband who didn't absorb her interest. They didn't have the opposition of their work. She had children she could leave with her husband and his sisters and their families, and the children were satisfied to be left. They had school and clubs and friends and activities. They hardly had time to talk on the phone to Winnie. Or to text. Their fingers were busy snapping letters to their friends about the most inconsequential things. What a waste of messaging. Winnie hungered for more than the disposable. Where were the messages of her father about eternal things? God and Christ and the Holy Ghost and their lives in relation to them? She remembered Grandma Winifred expounding on the Bible while her mother looked at the wall behind her.

The Figgetts came from Fenton to see what they wanted for their Art and Cultural Center. Winnie talked them into taking more ziggurats for the archives. Maybe someday someone would discover Eugena's work. They could be the executors of the ziggurats. They declined.

Winnie read her mother's journals. She would take the eight volumes. Maybe she could keep the house as a museum. Hold soirées on Sunday afternoons. Didn't she remember running through the house while her parents read *The Divine Comedy*? Winnie saw her mother's ziggurat journals as historical art. Maybe she could get an official historical landmark to put by the road.

Winnie woke discouraged in the mornings in her parent's decrepit house. She was no longer a girl in the backseat between brothers—Daniel taunting Warren, whisking his arm across her to poke Warren. If she slapped his arm away, she was the one who got in trouble. How could parents be so blind? Why didn't they know what a little goat they had for a son? She and Lizbet had run from the boys. Then Warren, Thomas, and John II joined the girls in running from Daniel. Had Daniel's trouble been their fault? Weren't they the first ones who made him feel like he was someone no one wanted to be with? Had he been marked separate from them from the beginning? He was the oldest. He should have led. But he was a follower. A taunter. A breaker into whatever game they played—not to play with them or add an older interest to his younger siblings and cousins, but to disrupt, to take away. To belittle. When Uncle John and Aunt Thelma came for a visit, it was a time for sparring—not playing, as long as Daniel was there, but a journey into some ancient game of survival. Daniel was the bear. He was the giant. He was the enemy from which they fled. He never knew how to play games with them. He was always the force moving against them. Did one of them cry at his death? Warren did, Winnie remembered, but it was tears of anger at the hurt that Daniel had caused him as a boy. Her father was lost in his thoughts of God. Her mother with her zigguratty thoughts. Had her parents built their distant worlds to escape their children? Would they have been better off without them? Frank and Eugena had had their separate worlds in the same house. They shared their alternate universes at meals. The children were moons or tertiary bodies.

"All their talk about heaven and hell stilled us," Winnie said as she talked to Lizbet. "What did we have that was comparable? What could we have said that would take their attention away from their debates?"

"Daniel found a way. Drugs," Lizbet stated.

"Warren found a way. Science and his online work. So did John II and Thomas. Their work absorbs them. What do we have?"

"Our families," Lizbet said. "What a strange question."

Well, that was the answer, Winnie discovered. Time moves on. Messes are cleared up, or moved away from, or become inconsequential with the passing of time, or return.

"I tell you, sometimes I think I hear Eugena. I hear her more than Frank, who left less rubbish behind. He had his affairs more in order."

Warren had come to the house with his children, Frank and Lilly, and Carol, his wife.

"Our father had the floor. He was a minister, after all. Our mother spoke too. But mainly there was the remoteness of her work shed. I hope the hereafter for her is a work shed," Winnie said. "The words "mom" and "dad" are palindromes—words that could be read the same backward and forward. Such central names to our survival," Winnie explained. "I think of them in the same way—only vertical instead of horizontal words."

"What do you mean?" Warren asked.

"Frank in heaven. Eugena in hell," Winnie answered. "Him working with the sky. Her working with the clay of the earth."

"How can you say that?" Warren asked. "They are in the same place. I'm sure they're sitting somewhere with Daniel between them. Why do you think there's a heaven and hell?"

"Mother had her own books too, among her journals," Winnie said to change the subject. "Herodotus. Thucydides. The old historians. Her own copy of Dante. A Bible with spotted pages. Why hadn't she taken better care of her books?"

"So they could turn to dust like my father's?" Warren said.

"Our father's," Winnie corrected. "She left piles of clay-making journals. Pottery. What will I do with all her art? Fenton's library doesn't want the books or any more of her ziggurats.

After Dad died, Mother tried to get Dad's college to come and get his books along with his massive collection of papers."

"Should we have a fire?" Warren asked. Had she found insurance papers in their parents' belongings? Had she made any progress at all?

"If the Figgetts at the Art and Cultural Center of Fenton would take a load of her ziggurats . . . " Winnie cut him off.

"If, if, if—"

Aunt Thelma and Uncle John had not left this kind of mess for their children.

Winnie sat in the kitchen with her brother and his family. Outside, where they had played as children, their voices still seemed to curl in the leaves.

Grant and the children came for the weekend. They brought schoolbooks and sat at the kitchen table where Winnie herself had sat while she tried to work as her parents talked about faith. None of that conversation was in her family. Was she responsible for it not being? The children loved to look through the house, opening drawers, looking into closets for old clothes and whatever caught their attention.

"Finish another page of your homework," Winnie said. "Read another chapter in the book and you can get up."

Grant sat at the table bored, and soon returned to his laptop.

Warren and his family had moved to the hotel in Fenton. Carol couldn't stand the old smell of the house anymore. When they came on Sunday, the first event was a trip to the cemetery.

"Sometimes I hear their voices."

"I don't," Warren said. "What can you say about our childhood? We were auxiliaries to our parents."

"I had the same feeling. We were satellite dishes floating above the earth while they led their lives—mainly orbiting around Daniel."

"Have you really found where you belong?" Warren asked. "Have you found your work shed or the chair in your study where the whole world moved before you?"

"I don't look at it that way," Winnie said. "They had a privileged life not everyone has. Who knows how they got it? They had a time and opportunity that fit them. The world has changed."

"Has it?"

"We have to work. We can't always have whatever we're suited for."

"Yes, I have to work," Warren said. "I can't preach. I teach college physics. I'm barely holding onto my contract. I'm struggling with publication. I can't find exactly where I want to focus my research."

"We didn't have a house we could move into like they did. It came to them through family," Winnie said. "We have a mortgage. I assume you do too. Ziggurats don't appeal to me. I couldn't do what Eugena did."

"It's what I'm looking for," Warren told me. "I need something that absorbs my interest. I need to get lost in ziggurats. Maybe there's a structure in the cosmos they followed. Frank rooted in the Bible. Eugena in ziggurats. Maybe if I keep thinking—"

That evening, Winnie sat in her mother's work shed. The smell of clay and dirt was overwhelming. She saw the crooked shelves. The disheveled table. The boxes and bins of found objects for the ziggurats. The window glass had a small crack in it. The vines outside were working their way into the crack. Winnie sat on the bench trying to imagine whole days in the shed out of sight. Whole days shaping clay into ziggurats. Winnie saw the buckets that had held water as if Eugena were still working there. The kiln that was a little work of hell.

Maybe her mother needed a retreat. She created the work shed as a reason for leaving the house. Where else did she have to go? Eugena loved the barren stretches of land. She loved the ocean for the same reason, though she'd never been out on it, as far as Winnie knew. Maybe her mother had other secret places. Winnie couldn't think where. Her mother seemed anchored on their acreage east of Fenton. That's what the relator called it, "acreage." Possibly to focus on the land and not the house, garage, and work shed, which were in need of repair. But it was her property now. Hers and Warren's. What would they do? Would Warren want to move here? Couldn't he work from home with physics courses online? He could move his family. Winnie and Grant could move here. The children would protest. No one wanted to be uprooted from school and friends and activities to head into the unknown, at least not until college. The lives of her parents were located in one place. The lives of Winnie and her brother and their families did not seem situated. They could live in any of a number of houses in the same area as the high school where their children went. Winnie felt like she needed a plan. But the days of plans were over. They had to go where the work was. They had to worry about bills. Maybe her parents had also, but she never knew it.

But did her mother have choices? She was married to a minister. Winnie remembered their lives on the front row of church. What had her mother been thinking as they listened to her father? Was she taking it in? Were the ziggurats her little towers of rebellion? Did she shut out his voice? Maybe she had less interest in her marriage than Winnie. Was her parents' marriage unhappy? No. They were different people with a purpose to be with one another in their differences. It held them together, while differences seemed to separate Winnie and Grant.

Why wasn't Winnie infecting her family with Scripture the way her father did? It was nonexistent in Warren's life too, as far as Winnie knew. "Our mission in life is to know the Father"—that was Frank's voice. But there were so many things in the way. How did her father keep his attention on God? Did he ever have his head out of the Bible? There was the voice of her mother Winnie heard in her head. There was the voice of her father. Maybe

Eugena clung to Frank's family for the comfort they offered. But was Eugena comfortable? This work shed was where she must have found comfort. It's where she went. Maybe it was not as dirty when she was in it. Maybe it was only dusty. Had Eugena ever allowed Mrs. Woodruff in the work shed to dust? Had the work shed ever seen a vacuum cleaner? Had the little roar of the machine ever rattled its walls? Not that Winnie knew. Look at the ziggurats. They had been shaped by Eugena's hands and hardened in the pit of hell—the little squat hog of a kiln. This was her butchering shed. Didn't Grandmother Winnie have a butchering shed on the farm? What would Winnie do with all the ziggurats? She went to the grocer's in Fenton for boxes. She would take some of the ziggurats to her house. Store them in the garage or basement. She had to keep some remnant of her mother's work. Would Warren want any of them? Would his wife, Carol? No, Warren was already burdened with college politics, classes, and committee work. Who knew what their lives were like? Winnie had spent most of her life with Warren and had no idea what he was thinking. What were his concerns? His fears? But Daniel had taught them to keep their feelings to themselves. They had to understand his behavior. They were not free to judge. Daniel had problems. He had issues. He was the one who absorbed all the attention until his parents had no more attention to give. But Daniel was someone she was not allowed to get angry at. Daniel had to be protected. She still felt she didn't matter.

One Christmas, Winnie's parents had given her a watch. It was gone after a few weeks. Her mother asked where she had lost it, implying it had been her fault. "Why didn't you just give it straight to Daniel?" Winnie screamed at her mother in frustration and rage. "Then he wouldn't be guilty of stealing!"

How many times were there like that? Daniel, the front-runner. The rest of us had to stay behind.

"We did matter," Warren told Winnie. "It's taken me years to think that way. Look who is still here?"

"Yes, Daniel even got out of having to clean up the parents' place," Winnie said.

"He missed out on a lot of things. Fatherhood. Responsibility. Taxes."

"The realtor mentioned a garage sale. I didn't tell her that Daniel took most of what could be sold."

"He's still dominating our conversation," Warren commented.

"Yes, but he's not here, is he?"

"His children could be playing with ours."

"Maybe I should find a craft like Mother," Winnie said. "A cottage industry is the way to earn a living in this economy."

"You can't be serious," Warren said. "What did Eugena ever earn? Ziggurats are limited in what they bring in."

"So it seems. Maybe Grant could design a web page. Maybe a dealer would take an interest. Maybe they could be featured."

"I'm for getting rid of the stuff. Hiring some workers from Fenton to gut the house," Warren decided. "It's a large old house. Think what it would look like restored."

"Do you have money for that?" Winnie asked.

"Then let's just auction it as-is—stuff and all," Warren changed his mind.

"I think an auction is piece by piece. Furniture. Dishes. Kitchen utensils and cutlery. Tables. Chairs. Books and books."

"Who would want the books?" Warren asked.

"Roland Muskee took a few, but even he was overwhelmed and refused to take any more. Second-hand dealers. Used bookstores. Frank stuck letters in the pages. He collected old stamps and kept them in the pages. I don't have time to go through each book off the shelf."

"The skillet has to be thrown away," Carol said. "I couldn't cook in it. I could hardly find a pot or pan that wasn't still dirty after Eugena washed it. I looked at the bedding and there is hardly a sheet or pillow case that is not thin, worn, and stained."

"I don't want people nosing through our parents' soiled bedding," Winnie said. "What do you think the mattresses look like?"

"A dumpster for that sort of thing," Warren said dejectedly.

"Do you know what that costs?" Grant asked.

Ziggurats for Sale

Houses were moving east from Fenton. A developer bought the acreage. He would tear down the house, the garage, the work shed. He would mow the field and build a suburb and name it "Fenton Heights." One day Warren and Winnie would drive by and not see any evidence of where their parents' house had been. Other children would be playing in the yard. There would be sidewalks. Houses built side by side. The mailbox would be attached to the house. A mailman would walk between the houses and place mail neatly in the slot of each front door.

Frank in Heaven

HEAVEN A ZIGGURAT? A ziggurat! If Eugena could see. It is as it was written in the Bible. But what was written? Not much. Not this. Heaven and heaven. The glory is glorious. So glorious you can't stop falling on your face. The stories go on and on. The levels grow smaller as they rise into heaven. It's the form Eugena worked with all her life—one terrace rising above another—yet she didn't see what it was about. Why didn't she know what she was making? Why didn't I? We are we blind. *Blind*. Even when we think we see. But when you are here, you fall on your face before *him*. It is glorious. *Glorious!* As far as you can see. It's more than can be believed. You try to stand—but you are falling down before Christ in worship, wonder, praise, relief.

www.ingramcontent.com/pod-product-compliance
Lightning Source LLC
Chambersburg PA
CBHW070907160426
43193CB00011B/1400